EXCUSE MY FRENCH!

STEVEN FAWKES

rs LLP, part of the Pearson Education Group

BBC logo © BBC 1996. BBC and BBC ACTIVE are trademarks of the British Broadcasting Corporation

First published 2006, reprinted 2006

Excuse My French is a RDF Media Group Plc Production for the BBC. © RDF Media Group Plc 2006. Licensed by RDF Rights. All rights reserved.

The right of Steven Fawkes to be identified as author of this Work has been asserted by him in accordance with the Copyright, Designs and Patents Act, 1988.

ISBN-10: 1-4066-1011-9
ISBN-13: 9-781406-61011-6

Printed by Canale, Italy

The Publisher's policy is to use paper manufactured from sustainable forests.

Commissioning editor: Debbie Marshall
Project editor: Melanie Kramers
Senior production controller: Man Fai Lau

BOOK
Concept design: Pentacor book design
Cover design: gray318
Cover/inside illustrations: Andy Davies/ Eyecandy
Consultant: Pauline Swanton
Editor: Sue Purcell
Designer: Rob Lian

DVD
DVD designed and authored by Arias UK
Producer: Saira Bhatti
Designer: Danny Law
Audio producer: Martin Williamson, Prolingua Productions
Studio: The Audio Workshop
Voices: Juliet Danté, Yves Aubert, Steven Fawkes

RDF team
Executive producer: Jamie Simpson
Series producer: Madeleine Hall
Producer/Director: Zizi Durrance
Producer/Director: Emma Jessop
Production executive: Janne Read
Commissioning editor: Maxine Watson

With thanks to …
Institut Français, London: (Director of Language Centre) Francis Hetroy
The teachers: Thierry Gauthier, Patricia Gaudron, Christine Purel
The celebrities: Esther Rantzen, Ron Atkinson, Marcus Brigstocke
Director of consumer products: Mark Lesbirel
Business affairs executives: Conrad Mewton, Fiona McGarrity
Product manager RDF Rights: Laura Owen
The team at RDF Rights.
ALL (Association for Language Learning)

Contents

Introduction

This book is for tourists and holiday-makers travelling in France, encountering the sort of 'challenges' the celebrities meet in the *Excuse My French!* TV programmes when trying to communicate in French. The main focus of the book is on dealing with some of these issues: making a start, developing strategies for coping, and particularly on speaking and understanding what people say, using the French you do know and all of the other communication skills you have.

As you'll see in the programmes, making mistakes is part of the process of rising to the challenge! But the key messages are: give it a go, don't take your mistakes too seriously, get over them and get on with it. After all, Ron manages to get on well with the people he meets in the footballing world, in spite of never having learned French before, and Marcus overcomes dyslexia and anxiety to perform in French on the stage.

The book is divided into six broad Themes, as real life is messier than precise topics! There are links between the Themes, as well as strategies for coping and for learning the sort of French you might personally need, as well as links to the DVD, especially to train your ear and keep your mouth under control!

Using the DVD

As well as the complete *Excuse my French!* programmes, the DVD contains additional material and challenges to give you practice in speaking and listening to French. It also has an audio Toolkit to help you work out the crucial area of pronunciation. Whenever you see the symbol below in your book, it means there is linked content in the Interactive section of the DVD.

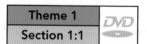

Section 1: Video clips	Section 3: Try it out
Section 2: Audio clips	Section 4: DVD challenge

The DVD allows you to watch subtitles in French or English, helping you get into the detail of the spoken French. At first, you may want to watch the programmes through with the 'translation of French' switched on, so that you can really get a feel for what the celebrities are going through, not to mention the funny mistakes they make when struggling to express themselves! Getting it wrong is something that happens to everyone, and is nothing to be surprised or embarrassed by. The struggle is an essential part of making progress, and with a language it really is true that you learn from making mistakes.

When you're feeling more confident, you can choose to watch without any subtitles to help tune your ear into the rhythms and flow of spoken French. Listening to French is even more effective when you actually see the people speaking in their local environment, not only because it adds a cultural context, but because you can really get a feel for common idioms, key expressions and all the different ways in which they're used.

As an additional learning tool, switch on the French subtitles ('all speech') so that you can pinpoint these key words and expressions by seeing them written down. With a little experimentation, you'll soon find a way of using the subtitles that suits you.

What's different about this book?

The book takes the celebrities' experiences in Provence as a basis for giving common-sense strategies to help you cope in your encounters with French people, in typical holiday situations, and in applying the French you already know to different circumstances. These strategies include:

• Taking responsibility

It's up to you to take the initiative, to take the first step, to be assertive and to take any opportunities that come your way. Only you can decide what you want to learn, what you don't need to know just yet, and how you learn and practise French. There is a range of learning styles to choose from – try different strategies until you find a way that works for you. Share your problems and successes to keep a sense of progress.

• Thinking about the culture

Politeness, body language and humour can all make or break a conversation with a French person. Don't forget that jokes and etiquette work differently in French!

• Coping

In real life, people don't follow a script, and communication can be pretty random; try to use what you know, and recognise all the possible means there are of getting your message across (not just through speech). Work out strategies: for establishing a safe start to a conversation, for checking you've understood something correctly, or have been understood, for recycling language you already know and for picking up new French from what's going on around you. Think about the key points you need to understand when spoken to (and what you can probably ignore).

• Understanding the big differences

A sense of how French works will let you make up, and say, new sentences more spontaneously. Use 'The big differences' sections to get to grips with some of the basics.

• Making new language

Use the Language Wheels to identify some frequently-used French, applicable to a variety of situations, and make up your own sentences. As only you know the specialised French you need to learn (dependent on your personal interests and plans) look up this vocabulary using your own preferred resource, or some of the free websites suggested on page 6.

• Having not so great expectations

Be realistic about how much time you have to devote to learning French, and what you can actually hope to achieve in that time. You can't expect to become fluent in French in a month, but you can expect to be able to communicate. Focus on what you really need to learn how to say. It's more than likely you'll get frustrated, plateau, and, in particular, make mistakes. Remember that it isn't all about getting it right, but about getting on, and don't worry excessively! You will meet many ways of saying the same thing in French; although you can try to recognise them all, you only need to use the one you like best. Keep your goals realistic.

Use the book, the DVD, the on-line resources and your other materials at your own pace; remember to have a break and ...
amusez-vous bien! *(have fun!)*

Resources

Excuse My French! **aims to help you make a start in learning French that is relevant to you. It will get you thinking about your priorities, what language you personally need, and how to cope in real-life situations. Once you've got the confidence to make that start, you'll want to go further, and there are lots of good resources available to help you.**

The BBC Languages website offers a wide range of free resources to help you improve your French. Visit www.bbc.co.uk/languages to find out more.

- There's a dedicated *Excuse My French!* area where you'll find some quickfire interactive challenges linked to the programmes at the levels of the three celebrities: www.bbc.co.uk/languages/french/excusemyfrench.

- *French Steps* is an online course for complete beginners where you'll also find a useful pronunciation guide (as well as tips on grammar): http://www.bbc.co.uk/languages/french/lj/pronunciation/.

- The new interactive broadband video material in *Ma France* gives an insight into real people's lives: www.bbc.co.uk/languages/french/mafrance.

- *Talk French* is a lively video-based introduction to French – a TV series and book are also available: www.bbc.co.uk/languages/french/talk/.

- *Le Mensuel* is a monthly audio magazine for intermediate level learners: www.bbc.co.uk/languages/french/news/.

And there's more … learn cool French and slang expressions, as well as essential holiday phrases, and share funny holiday blunders and advice with other learners.

There's a wide range of other languages also on offer, including Spanish, Italian, Greek, German, Portuguese and Mandarin Chinese.

- CILT, the national centre for languages, has information on everything to do with languages, from finding a course in your area, to advice on using languages at work. You can explore your options at: www.cilt.org.uk/.

- The celebrities were taught by teachers from the Institut Français. As well as learning French on one of their courses, you can improve your knowledge of French wine, cinema and society. To find out more, visit: www.institut-francais.org.uk/.

- The Association for Language Learning can also point you in the direction of interesting events and activities: www.ALL-languages.org.uk/.

- Another useful site is www.linguanet-europa.org, which covers all European languages. Test your level, try out a range of different courses, get advice on keeping motivated, and chat on-line with language-learners across Europe.

BBC Active is not responsible for the content of any third-party websites.

1

Getting going

Be kind to yourself

Learning how to speak another language is a big job. It takes time, self-confidence and some brainpower, and you'll undoubtedly make a lot of mistakes along the way. Why do people put themselves through all this? And what can you do to minimise the stress?

The point is that you will be able to do things and have experiences that are off limits for someone who only knows English. You'll be confident when dealing with other people, their culture and language. You'll soon realise that you don't need to worry about getting the right ending on every word every time, so don't let that fear put you off from even starting. Just don't expect to get it right first time. And don't think you can be as fluent, witty, wise and spontaneous in French in a matter of weeks as you are in the language you've been speaking all your life! But if you stick at it you will succeed.

The three celebrities in the programmes on the DVD go through the same ups and downs as thousands of other language learners. We see them:

* working out what's important to learn
* doing tasks they don't see the relevance of
* dealing with real people and their personalities
* wanting to reach further than they're able to
* reaching a plateau
* and falling out with the teacher!

Their experiences help them discover what factors lead to success. If you bear all these points in mind, it will take the worry and stress out of learning, and help you feel up to taking the challenge. They learn that you should:

- set yourself realistic targets
- celebrate your successes
- think (and then laugh) about the things that go wrong
- find a way to learn that suits you
- be brave and give it a go.

| Theme 1 | DVD |
| Section 1:1 | |

One thing that's clear from the programmes on the DVD is that a challenge really does focus the attention! During Ron's attempt at being a wine waiter, he progresses from being incomprehensible to successfully taking an order. In the same programme, however, we see Esther getting hugely frustrated by her job as head waitress. So, why the difference between Ron and Esther? Ron is actually interested in wine; we know that from his antics on the guided tour of the haunts of the rich and famous in Saint-Tropez! Esther, on the other hand, sees no link between her journalistic work and playing at restaurants for the day. So, when you set yourself a challenge, make sure it is something you really want (or need) to be able to do.

YOUR FIRST CHALLENGE: WHAT'S YOUR STYLE?

In the programmes, the teachers talk about the 'immersion method' of learning French. This means spending time hearing and speaking only French, without the fallback of explanations in English. It's considered a more natural environment – you learn how to use the language in context, rather than examine its workings in theory. After all, you don't need to be a mechanic to drive a car; it's enough to be able to make it take you where you're going. The same goes for French; the key thing is to know enough French to let you do what you want – buy things, find your way, make friendly conversation – but you don't need to know all the whys and wherefores.

The immersion technique is not a style that suits everyone and if you feel uncomfortable with it, don't worry. You'll meet other ways of rehearsing, coping with and learning French in the rest of this book. These include:

- writing things down
- joining things up
- using what you've got
- avoiding word-for-word translation
- following the words on screen
- making friends with your dictionary
- acting it out

and most useful of the lot, because it's inevitable:
- getting it wrong.

Understanding a bit about how things in the language work can be very helpful, especially when you want to say something you're pretty sure you haven't learned as a set phrase or sentence. When you're trying to generate language that is original (to you, at least) an appreciation of the tools and skills you already have can help enormously. In each Theme of this book, look out for 'The big differences' sections, which explain the key differences in how French and English work. The Language Wheels in 'Making your own language' will show you how to construct your own sentences, and you can find out more about the nuts and bolts of the language in the Toolkit at the back of the book.

Theme 1	
Section 1:2	

The teachers encourage the celebrities to speak French all day (or at least until 6pm). This is particularly tough for Ron with his limited French, but he doesn't let that stop him. Playing to his strengths, he works out his own coping strategies. Watch this video clip of a rainy day trip to Avignon, and notice how Ron manages to make a joke at Esther's expense, through expression and tone of voice.

GETTING IN SHAPE FOR SPEAKING

French you didn't know you knew

Recognise these words?

Information	Organisation	Exploration
Imagination	Migration	Communication
Nation		

They're all words that exist in both English and French. Written down, they may look the same, but when spoken they sound completely different. You need to tune in to the way they are pronounced and stressed in French, and expect that your mouth (which is used to speaking English) will feel quite different when speaking French!

In English the stress in longer words is not always in the same place. Words of three syllables sometimes have the stress on the
1st: *robb*-ery   2nd: migr-*a*-tion   or 3rd syllable: Japan-*ese*.

In French the stress is nearly always on the last syllable, however long the word is. So, an English speaker stresses the penultimate -a- syllable in all of these words – try it out loud or in your head – while a French speaker stresses the final ***-tion*** syllable. Before you try that, remember that the French sound and spelling systems are different too; it's not only a matter of stress. When you've read this section, listen to the DVD to hear the words said by French speakers and then force your mouth to behave in the French way.

Theme 1
Section 2:1 DVD

information
imagination
nation
organisation
migration
exploration
communication

Communication is what it's all about! And as you speak English, you already have a large vocabulary in French, as long as you pronounce it the French way – stress on the last syllable.

Making new language

It's all very well in the early stages to learn a few set phrases by heart, but you can never expect to learn all of the phrases, constructions or vocabulary you will actually need in every situation. You can prepare yourself, though, for when you'll need to invent your own!

The celebrities soon realise that being immersed in French, deep in rural Provence, is pretty exhausting, as conversations can go in any direction. You have to expect the unexpected! Real-life communication can be unpredictable – conversations don't necessarily follow the pattern they do in textbooks. The key to success is being able to transfer the language you do know into new situations – recycling it, so to speak. Within any language there are certain words and phrases that work harder than others – they're used more, they're more versatile. These are the words and phrases you'll want to make your top priority when learning French.

One example is *Il y a* which means 'there is' or 'there are', and, with just a change in your voice, it can also be a question – 'Is there ...?', 'Are there ...?'.

Il y a un marché à Gordes. *There's a market in Gordes.*
Il y a un marché à Gordes? *Is there a market in Gordes?*
Il y a des toilettes ici? *Are there any toilets here?*

Il y a is an especially useful phrase when exploring a new town. You'll often hear *près d'ici?* (*nearby*) on the end. For example, *Il y a un golf près d'ici?* (*Is there a golf course nearby?*).

And of course, as French is the language of etiquette, there should be a *s'il vous plaît* (*please*) after that as well! Look at the Language Wheel on the next page, and think when and where you might ask the questions. Then try saying all seven sentences in full (including the *près d'ici* and *s'il vous plaît* where appropriate – it's a good habit to get into). Make them a question by making your voice rise towards the end. You can hear them on the DVD.

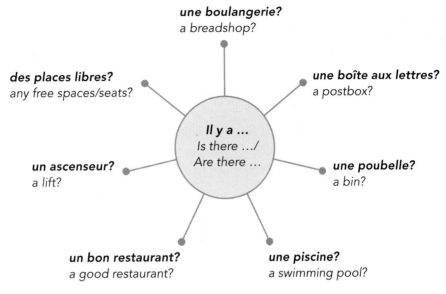

Theme 1	DVD
Section 2:2	

une boulangerie?
a breadshop?

des places libres?
any free spaces/seats?

une boîte aux lettres?
a postbox?

Il y a ...
Is there .../
Are there ...

un ascenseur?
a lift?

une poubelle?
a bin?

un bon restaurant?
a good restaurant?

une piscine?
a swimming pool?

TRY IT OUT

There is more about asking questions in Theme 3. To prove you can do it yourself, make up some questions or statements of your own, adapting the examples in the Language Wheel, if that helps, and using a dictionary or phrasebook for extra words. The point is to get used to creating your own French sentences, based on things you might want to say. This is just a practice activity, so don't worry too much about your sentences being entirely sensible!

Theme 1	DVD
Section 2:3	

So, to start you off, how could you ask:

1 if there's a car park nearby?

2 if there's a hospital nearby?

3 if there's a cinema nearby?

4 if there's a discount for children?

You can see suggested answers at the back of the book, and hear them on your DVD.

un parking *car park*

un hôpital *hospital*

un cinéma *cinema*

un tarif réduit *discount*

pour les enfants *for children*

WRITE IT DOWN

A lot of people feel they need to write things down in order to learn or remember them. This can be a useful learning activity in itself, as long as you are clear about what you are writing and why you are writing it. Remember that simply copying a list of disconnected items of vocabulary will almost certainly:

- not help you remember the individual words
- not help you find them again in a hurry
- not be much fun!

but writing down words:

- that you really like the sound of
- that are in a word bank on a specific theme (e.g. a special interest)
- that come up very frequently
- that are useful to keep the flow of conversation going

can be really worth it.

JOIN THINGS UP

Instead of writing long lists, you could organise words and phrases you want to remember in a 'Language Map'. This suits people whose visual and spatial memory is particularly strong, and who remember things according to how they are set out. A Language Map can be useful for grouping together words, expressions and concepts that you associate with each other or that are personal to you. For example, for a theme like 'talking about yourself', a map could start from a mental tour of your home and the area around it. Starting with the very personal, the first reference point could be the bathroom mirror. As you look at it, think through some French you could use about yourself:

Je m'appelle ... *My name is ...*
Je viens de ... *I come from ...*
J'habite à ... *I live in ...*

You could then continue:

Je suis marié(e). *I'm married.*
J'ai deux/trois/six enfants. *I have 2/3/6 children.*

This is the departure point for your Language Map. When you think 'bathroom mirror' you should start to think **Je m'appelle ...**, **Je viens de ...** and so on.

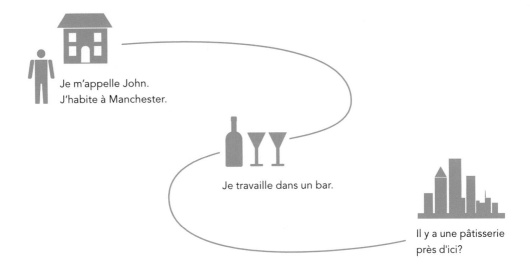

Je m'appelle John.
J'habite à Manchester.

Je travaille dans un bar.

Il y a une pâtisserie
près d'ici?

Your next place on your map could be where you work, or the local shop, or the garden, the school, the town centre, a restaurant or pub. Pick somewhere that's important to you and then store a bit of useful French with your picture of the place to create a useful memory hook.

If it's the place you work, you might have:

Je suis professeur/journaliste/analyste/pianiste. *I'm a teacher/journalist/analyst/pianist.*

Je travaille dans un bar/un bureau. *I work in a bar/an office.*

Theme 1	DVD
Section 2:4	

Listen to all these sample sentences on the DVD to help polish your spoken French. Note the versatility of the phrase **Je suis** (*I am*). It can be used to give your marital status, your job, or even your name: **Je suis Eleanor** (*I'm Eleanor*).

In your mental picture of the town centre you might also store some of the **Il y a** questions from above, so that you'll remember when you're in a town in France how to ask if there is a cake shop nearby. (It could be a lifesaver!) **Il y a une pâtisserie près d'ici?** (*Is there a cake shop nearby?*).

Your Language Map doesn't have to be written down, you could just remember certain pieces of French in your head as a loosely connected series of places. The point is to make the places in your map, as well as the French you want to use, entirely personal – only you know the kind of things you do, or want to, say.

If the idea of a Language Map appeals, you can create one on other themes – shopping, for instance, in which case you'd jot down words and phrases for things you want to buy. You can look up relevant words in a dictionary, phrasebook, or via the free on-line resources listed on page 6.

Theme 1	DVD
Section 3	

USING WHAT YOU'VE GOT

One thing to think about is how you're going to use your word lists and Language Maps when you've created them. There's no point having the neatest lists in the world if you never look at them! One good way for many people is to see, practise and use a newly-learned piece of language several times within a short timescale. So, say your new phrase is **On y va?** *(Shall we go? – one of the celebrities' most-used phrases!)*, you might want to do some or all of these:

- listen to it on the DVD
- look at how it's written
- write it down
- say it in your head
- say it out loud
- remember what it means.

Ten minutes or so later you might do the same things again. An hour or so later you might just:

- say it in your head
- say it out loud
- remember what it means.

If you like to see how things are written you might try to write it again, but the spelling is not always helpful to everyone in remembering how to say it. Later that day you might check on it again, and then start to try to use it as often as possible in real life.

Be kind to yourself

READING

Although it may seem logical that listening is the best way for you to improve your speaking – you hear the sounds and patterns and can copy them – reading French is also very useful. Reading expands your knowledge of French, sometimes without you realising it. In a French street you'll notice signs, posters and adverts, which can reveal a lot about the culture of the place, but also provide language that you may find yourself using in the future. Within this book you'll find dialogues and other texts in French.

Valuable sources of additional language, these can be used in various ways: recognising words you already know, guessing the meaning of others (from the context, or because they look like other words you know) and learning new, specialist words that strike you as important, either because they come up a lot, or because they relate to a topic you're interested in.

TRY IT OUT

Look at this French web page, showing train and travel requirements, and a journey planner.

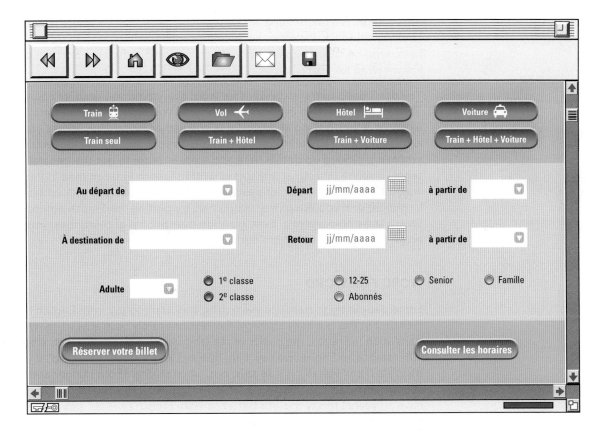

You can see that the key words are illustrated by images, and that it is not unlike a British train company's site. These are all clues you can use to work out the language. Scan around the page, and pick out the following:

Train + hotel + car
Leaving from …
Going to …
Next, work out what jj/mm/aaaa might stand for.

You can see the answers at the back of the book.

You'll see words that are similar to English ones, and you'll spot patterns – that **consulter** *(to consult)* and **réserver** *(to reserve)* are giving instructions and both end in **-er**, and that an ^{e} next to a number is the equivalent of -st, -nd, -th (**première**, first, **deuxième**, second). You may be able to recall some of these words in French next time you need to recognise or say them.

Pause for thought

Although guessing is an essential part of language learning, you can't always assume you know the meaning of new words you come across – look them up! When travelling by train in France an Englishman stepped out at a small rural station. His phone rang – it was his wife calling to see where he was. Looking round the platform, he announced that he had just arrived at 'Sortie'. Let's hope he wasn't expecting her to come and pick him up. **Sortie** is the French word for *'Exit'*.

You don't need to translate word for word everything you read, of course. Think of how you read in English; sometimes you are scouring for detail, for example, when looking at a timetable or weather report; sometimes you are just scanning a page until something catches your eye; sometimes you are skimming, picking up details here and there in order to get the general sense. If you're looking at any sort of written French you can read in the same way. If the subject matter interests you, you're more likely to pick up bits of language, so if you like glossy magazines, try getting the French editions from a large newsagent's. Even glancing over photos of celebrities, you'll acquire new vocabulary from the captions.

WORD FOR WORD

Some people try to translate everything they want to say from English to French, but this is a risky strategy. Expressions rarely have a word-for-word translation in French; the basics of the language are quite different, after all. For instance, in English we say 'I am hungry', and 'I am 30 years old'. If you translate *'I am'* literally, it's **Je suis**, but, when talking about hunger and age, French uses **J'ai faim** (literally, *'I have hunger'*) and **J'ai 30 ans** (literally, *'I have 30 years'*) to say this. It's better to learn French phrases and idioms in their entirety, rather than look up individual words in French and try to cobble together a sentence.

Literal translations can lead to faux pas. For example, if you look up the word 'full' in a dictionary, you'll find **plein**, but this is only when talking about objects such as boxes, suitcases etc. So, after a good meal it would not be wise for a woman to say to her generous hosts: **Merci beaucoup, maintenant je suis pleine**, as this actually means *'Thank you very much, I'm pregnant now!'*.

This is also why it's difficult to take jokes from English into French; too many words don't do exactly what you think, and punning jokes or words with double meanings in English almost never work in French.

A dictionary is a useful tool for language learners, but don't rely on it exclusively. The tips you'll find in the 'Make friends with your dictionary' sections of this book will help you use it effectively to say what you want to say.

GETTING IT WRONG

However you learn to speak another language (and there have been many methods over the years) one thing you can guarantee is that you're going to be making mistakes. It's inevitable, especially when you're trying to say things spontaneously, without time to check with your teacher, dictionary, or notes. So, what are you going to do about it? Accept it! Just get stuck in, have a go, and you'll find you learn as much, if not more, from finding a way to make yourself understood (even if it's not completely correct) than from not speaking out of anxiety that your verb endings are wrong.

Don't worry about getting it wrong; it's a natural part of the learning process – you may make a mistake this time, but you'll get it right the next!

READ IT, SAY IT

Mistakes in pronunciation often occur because people apply the English rules of pronunciation to French words (especially if they're written the same way). When you look things up in a dictionary, you need to think about the French rules, and get your mouth thinking how to pronounce them. Working up to a position where you can confidently look at a word and say it to your satisfaction is not an easy process, but the feel of French spoken well can be as delightful as the taste of the local produce!

The **-e-** sound in French, for example, is pretty consistent and is the sound in the word **le** (*the*), not that much different from the '-e' in the English word 'the'. Pronounce it like this unless:

- it has an accent: **-é-, -è-, -ê-**
- it is combined with another vowel (**-ei-, -eu-**) or it's followed by a consonant (**em-, -en, -ent, -ez, -et**).

Without knowing the rules of pronunciation, a very tricky word for the English speaker is **thé** (*tea*) – it just looks too much like one of the most common words in the English language. In fact it sounds quite different, as you'll hear, along with these other **-e-** sounds on the DVD.

One of the most important sounds in French is the famous 'e acute' – *é* – so called because of the angled acute accent. It's used all over the place, in **thé** and in words like **café**, **fiancé** and **risqué**, which are the same in English. It's used so frequently that you really should spend some time getting it right.

When you try to say it, remember it's a French sound – try changing the shape of your mouth, the position of your tongue and lips as you copy the sound until you find a position that makes the sound you're looking for. You'll be meeting 'e acute' a lot.

Words which end **-té** in French tend to end '-ty' in English. Listen to the DVD to hear all these words containing the 'e acute' sound pronounced. Then try to copy the sounds yourself.

Theme 1
Section 2:5

DVD

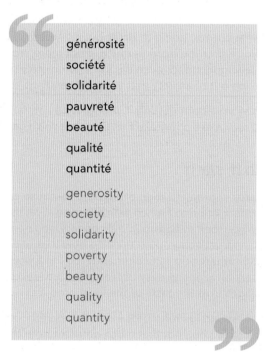

générosité

société

solidarité

pauvreté

beauté

qualité

quantité

generosity

society

solidarity

poverty

beauty

quality

quantity

In the Toolkit on page 126, you'll find a handy pronunciation guide to other key French sounds. You can hear all of these on the DVD, in Theme 1: Getting going (Audio clips 8-14).

Make friends with your dictionary

CONTROL YOUR MOUTH!

Matching writing to sound (being able to read aloud a new word in French that sounds right) is an essential skill for the avid dictionary or phrasebook user. You'll want to reach the stage where you can look up a word, find the one you want, and read and say it straight away, without holding up the flow of your conversation too much. The good news is that, as you've seen, there are lots of French words you'll recognise on sight. The not-so-good news is that, because they look so familiar, your mouth will immediately want to say them the English way! You will need to think consciously how to pronounce them, and gear up your mouth, tongue and teeth to do the job.

Theme 1	
Section 1:3	

Ron struggles with pronunciation – possibly because he's so keen on swotting up from books. Watch him trying to say the wine's aroma reminds him of *les épices* (*spices*). He knows the word, but his accent lets him down and he ends up in deep water. If there are things you're going to want to say often, make sure that you can pronounce them!

Making new language

Theme 1	
Section 1:4	

As you saw earlier, this is not as hard as it sounds, and is something you should aim to do as much as possible. It's what gives you the edge of confidence. Some pieces of language are indispensable – you hear them all the time, and you need to use them on a regular basis too. They can be adapted in hundreds of ways in different circumstances. *Vous avez ...?* is one such high priority piece of language because it's used in so many situations. It means *'Have you got ...?'*, *'Do you have ...?'* and *'Have you ...?'*. Watch this video clip and note how the celebrities use *Vous avez ...?* to ask questions in the tourist office.

Practise making up new French sentences – good preparation for when you're live in front of real French people! Look at this Language Wheel and try asking all seven questions, with your voice rising towards the end. You can hear the pronunciation on the DVD. *Vous avez* without a question mark means *'You have (got)'*.

Adding *s'il vous plaît* (*please*) to each sentence would make it sound more French. You can say this first, to attract someone's attention, in a similar way to *Excusez-moi* (*Excuse me*). If you put it at the end it completes the question politely. Try asking the questions aloud with *s'il vous plaît* at the beginning and the end to see which you find easier to say.

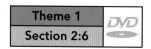

Theme 1
Section 2:6

un journal?
a newspaper?

un téléphone?
a phone?

des fleurs?
any flowers?

Vous avez ...
*Do you have .../
Have you
got ...*

des timbres?
any stamps?

un plan de la ville?
a town map?

des toilettes?
a toilet?

une chambre?
a room?

TRY IT OUT

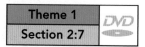

Theme 1
Section 2:7

You probably already have some ideas for other sentences you could invent using **Vous avez ...?**

So, why not create your own Language Wheel? To start you off, can you work out how to ask the following in French?

1 Have you got any children?

2 Have you got any oranges?

3 Have you got a car for me?

You can see suggested answers at the back of the book, and hear them on your DVD.

des enfants *(any) children*

des oranges *(any) oranges*

une voiture *car*

pour moi *for me*

The big differences

GENDER

You'll have noticed that some French words have **un** (a) or **le** (the) before them, and others **une** (a) or **la** (the).

un/le plan a/the map

un/le téléphone a/the telephone

une/la boulangerie a/the baker's

une/la piscine a/the swimming pool

Everyone knows that the French nation is famous for romance, style and everything to do with sex! Even their words are masculine (**un**) or feminine (**une**)! Is this just a plot to catch the English-speaking world out? Will they laugh at you if you get it wrong? And when is it important that you get it right?

French is not the only world language to use gender for its nouns – in fact, in not having them, English is one of the exceptions. The reason why some words are masculine and some feminine is due to French's Latin roots, and there is no universal, rational link between the meanings we attach to things and their gender. For instance, you can't generalise and say that everything to do with women will be feminine. So, everyone has feet that are masculine attached to legs that are feminine. Their fingers and thumbs are masculine, but are part of hands that are feminine.

Gender is something to be aware of (but not to panic about). For the most part, if you happen to say **une timbre** instead of **un timbre** (a stamp), people will understand what you mean. Some people will put you right, others won't bother. If you're worried about getting your **un** and **une** or **le** and **la** mixed up, you could always try to organise your word lists so that you can see which are which at a glance.

When you write new vocabulary down, try writing masculine nouns on the left-hand side of your paper, and feminine nouns on the right. Some people have a good memory for where things are placed, and find that when they think of the word, the memory of its position will trigger the right gender word too.

masculine	feminine
le café	la boulangerie
le restaurant	la pâtisserie
l'homme	la femme

If you are a person who learns by visualising, another tip is to use two different coloured pens when jotting down new nouns – a different colour for each gender.

Other people just get tuned in to the sound of the thing, or the feel of it in their mouth. Get into the habit of including the **le** or **la** when learning new vocabulary, as later on you'll find it comes naturally, and sounds right.

There are some patterns that can help you work out gender. Words ending in **-ation**, like the ones at the start of this Theme, are always feminine, as are words ending in **-euse** like **la photocopieuse** (photocopier), **-ette**, such as **la bicyclette** (bicycle), and the group of words ending in **-té** you saw earlier, like **société** (society) and **beauté** (beauty).

For more on gender see Toolkit, page 118

TRY IT OUT

From memory, work out whether these words are masculine or feminine. You could try organising them into columns, or, if you want to think bigger, writing them on post-its and reorganising them. Try the same exercise again later on to see if your remembering improves (or do it with another set of words). You can see the answers at the back of the book.

téléphone	voiture	marché	piscine
photocopieuse	cinéma	parking	chambre
journal	plan		

How do you know if it's **le** or **la**? Dictionaries always give this information, usually by writing an 'm' for masculine and an 'f' for feminine. Be aware that both **le** and **la** become **l'** before a vowel or silent 'h', so **un hôtel** (a hotel) is **l'hôtel** (the hotel) for instance.

Theme 1	
Section 4	

DVD Challenge

Time for an interactive challenge on the DVD! Try to complete it without notes. Once you've had a go you can review the answers, transcripts of all the French you've seen and the English translations at the back of the book.

DO	DON'T
– think about what it is you want to be able to do in French	– write a sheaf of notes and never look at it again
– be realistic	– be surprised if you make mistakes; you'll learn from them
– think about what you do with your mouth when speaking French	– hold back from trying out some new French you've invented
– try out different ways of rehearsing and learning	– give up!

2

Dealing with people

SETTING THE SCENE

It's a myth that French people, and especially Parisians, are rude and standoffish to foreigners on holiday. They probably do get a bit tired of giving out free tourist information, it's true, but the irony is that they think just the same about the British! What really gets on their **baguettes** is that British people don't say hello properly. The correct French way, especially in smaller towns and villages, is to greet everyone whose eye you meet, whether you know them or not, by wishing them **Bonjour!** *(Good morning!)*. This rule applies everywhere – in the street, in cafés and in shops – and will really help you to feel part of the local community.

Accompanying this with a smile or a nod of the head adds to the general feeling of well-being, as does tacking on **madame, mademoiselle**, or **monsieur**. In fact, you'll sometimes hear just the title, as a kind of shorthand for the full greeting (like saying 'Morning' instead of 'Good morning'). If there are several people, the proper old-fashioned way is to greet the women before the men. Nowadays, especially in a queue at the **boulangerie** *(baker's)*, you're more likely to hear the catch-all **Bonjour, messieurs-dames** *(Good morning, ladies and gentlemen)* as someone comes in. And when you leave the shop or café, you'll notice even more charm is spread around with a **merci** *(thank you)* and a **bonne journée** *(have a nice day)*.

Watch this clip to see how Esther and Marcus say hello and introduce themselves on their first day working in the restaurant.

Theme 2	DVD
Section 1:1	

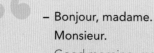

| Theme 2 |
| Section 2:1 |

How you greet people influences that all-important first impression. Look at the greetings below and then listen to them on the DVD. Have a go at saying them aloud yourself, trying to copy the sounds and rhythms you hear.

> – Bonjour, madame.
>   Monsieur.
> – Good morning, madam.
>   Morning, sir.
> – Bonjour, messieurs-dames.
>   Bonjour.
> – Good morning, ladies and gentlemen.
>   Good morning.
> – Bonjour, monsieur.
>   Mesdames, bonjour.
> – Comment allez-vous?
>   Très bien, et vous?
> – Bien, merci. Bonne journée.
>   Merci. Au revoir.
> – Good morning, sir.
>   Ladies, good morning.
> – How are you?
>   Very well, and you?
> – Fine, thank you. Have a nice day.
>   Thank you. Goodbye.
> – Bonjour, messieurs.
>   Bonjour, mademoiselle.
> – Vous allez bien?
>   Oui, merci. À bientôt!
> – Good morning, gentlemen.
>   Good morning, miss.
> – Are you well?
>   Yes, thank you. See you soon!

Comment allez-vous? (*How are you?*) is a polite enquiry you'll hear a lot, so is worth committing to memory. This phrase can be used in all situations, although you may hear variations such as: **Vous allez bien?** (*Are you well?*), **Comment ça va?** (*How's it going?*) (slightly less formal) and **Ça va?/Ça va bien?** (*Are you OK?*).

If someone asks you first, the classic response is first to reply to the question,

Bien, merci (Fine, thanks), then to return the query, *Et vous? (How about you?)*, rather like a ping pong game.

Comment allez-vous? How are you?
Bien merci, et vous? Fine thanks, and you?

Theme 2	DVD
Section 2:2	

TRY IT OUT

What greetings could you use in the following situations?

1 You walk into the local café, which is pretty full.

2 The barman catches your eye.

3 A young woman says *Bonjour* to you.

4 You pass two elderly women you see every day.

You can see the answers at the back of the book, and hear them on the DVD.

The big differences

VOUS AND TU

French, like many other languages, has different ways of saying 'you' depending on how well you know the person you are talking to. We used to do the same in English, with 'thou' or 'thee' and 'you' or 'ye'. Broadly speaking, you use the more formal *vous* for strangers, shopkeepers, and people older than yourself. Informal *tu* is for a friend, family member or a child – young people will usually use this to each other, even if they haven't met before. In order to avoid over-familiarity, and possibly causing offence, it's best to stick to the *vous* form, which is both economical (as it can also be used as a plural, for speaking to groups of people) and often easier to remember!

Theme 2	DVD
Section 2:3	

A typical formal exchange might go something like this. (You can hear both dialogues on your DVD, and see translations at the back of the book.)

" – Bonjour, madame.
Bonjour.
– Comment allez-vous?
Bien, merci, et vous?
– Bien, merci. Allez, à bientôt.
Au revoir et bonne journée. "

And you could also use these in less formal situations, no problem. An informal exchange might be:

" – Salut!
Bonjour!
– Ça va?
Oui, ça va, et toi?
– Bien, merci.
Ciao. "

For more on vous and tu see Toolkit, page 120

FIRST IMPRESSIONS

Theme 2	DVD
Section 2:4	

People are interested in other people, and want to know all about them. It's worth preparing a set piece to introduce yourself and your companions, to get that all-important first impression right. Picture the scene: waiting in a reception line at the ambassador's party …

> – Bonsoir, monsieur.
> Bonsoir.
> – Je me présente – je suis Roberta Evans et voici mon mari John.
> Enchanté de faire votre connaissance.
> – Enchantée. Bonne soirée.
>
> – Good evening.
> Good evening.
> – May I introduce myself – I'm Roberta Evans and this is my husband John.
> Pleased to make your acquaintance.
> – Very pleased to meet you. Have a lovely evening.

Even if you aren't invited to the ambassador's soirée, you'll still need to make introductions! Some of the words below may come in handy. One good way to remember them is by labelling a photograph, or sketching a rough family tree.

mon grand-père

moi

ma femme

ma belle-mère

ma fille

mon fils

Theme 2	DVD
Section 2:5	

Here are some other words you could use to talk about your family. You can hear how they sound on your DVD.

moi me

mon mari my husband

mon compagnon/ma compagne my partner

ma femme my wife

mon fils my son

ma fille my daughter

ma belle-mère my mother-in-law

mon grand-père my granddad

mes enfants my children

mes chiens my dogs

Theme 2	DVD
Section 1:2	

When introducing people, be careful how you word it! Watch this video clip of Esther's faux pas to find out what not to say.

The big differences

POSSESSIVE WORDS

In the word list above you'll have noticed different words for saying 'my'.

mon mari my husband

ma femme my wife

mes chiens my dogs

Why the difference? Again, it's because of gender; the word for 'my' changes to match the gender of the thing or person you are referring to – it has nothing to do with whether you are male or female. So, it's **mon** for masculine words such as **le mari**, **ma** for feminine words such as **la femme**, and **mes** for plurals, both masculine and feminine.

If you want to refer to someone else's family or possessions, use **votre** and **vos**, which both mean 'your'. Use **votre** before a singular word (masculine or feminine), and **vos** before a plural. The informal equivalents for 'your' are **ton** (masculine), **ta** (feminine), and **tes** (plural).

Theme 2	DVD
Section 2:6	

C'est votre femme? Is this your wife?

Oui, c'est ma femme. Yes, this is my wife

Ce sont vos enfants? Are these your children?

Oui, ce sont mes enfants. Yes, these are my children.

You can hear all these phrases on the DVD.

For more on possessive words see Toolkit, page 118

Theme 2	DVD
Section 3	

TRY IT OUT

Try out the language you've picked up so far in the interactive section of your DVD. You can see the answers, transcripts and translations at the back of the book.

MAKING CONVERSATION

Theme 2	DVD
Section 2:7	

Many simple conversations between strangers follow a pattern, and you can more or less predict what you'll be expected to say next. If you bump into the same people every day (at a hotel, in a village, in a shop) you're very likely to hear and say the same sorts of things. You could take either part of the following exchanges, passing the time of day and talking about the weather. Listen to them on your DVD.

> – Bonjour, madame.
> Bonjour.
> – Comment allez-vous?
> Bien, merci. *(The near universal answer!)*
>
> – Hello, madam.
> Hello.
> – How are you?
> Fine, thank you.
>
> – Ça va bien?
> Ça va. *(or Oui, merci.)*
>
> – Are you OK?
> I'm OK. *(or Yes, thank you.)*
>
> – Il fait beau aujourd'hui.
> Oui, n'est-ce pas?
>
> – The weather's nice today.
> Yes, isn't it?
>
> – Il ne fait pas beau aujourd'hui, hein?
> Oh non, alors.
>
> – The weather's not very nice today, is it?
> No, it's not.

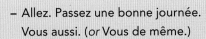

> – Allez. Passez une bonne journée.
> Vous aussi. (*or* Vous de même.)
> – Au revoir.
> À bientôt. (*or* À tout de suite/Salut/Au revoir.)
> – OK then, have a good day.
> You too. (*or* Same to you.)
> – Goodbye.
> See you soon. (*or* See you very soon (*i.e. straight away*)/
> Bye/Goodbye.)

Small extra words like **hein**, **eh bien**, **allez** and **alors** are the oil of any conversation, keeping it running smoothly. They are worth learning as they will make your French sound more authentic and natural, and also give you extra time to think about what to say next!

Hein? is a question you can use to get someone to repeat something (like *'eh?'* in English), to check if they agree with what you've just said, or whether you've got it right.
Le bus est à midi, hein? *The bus is at midday, isn't it?*
Alternatively, you can add **n'est-ce pas?** onto the end of the question, to mean *'isn't it?'/'right?'*.

Eh bien indicates hesitation, or that you are thinking about, or have given some thought to, the matter at hand.

Allez, as a throwaway word, is usually there to suggest that something is about to happen. In English we might say *'Right then'*.
Allez, bonne soirée. *Right then, have a nice evening.*

Alors is mostly used like *'so'*, *'well'* or *'right'* in English. You'll hear it quite a lot. As a question it's used to elicit information or an opinion. For example, if someone says **Alors?** to you in a shop, they're asking you what you want, or if you've made up your mind.

PUTTING PEOPLE AT EASE

How do you feel when people come up to you in the street to ask you something? Worried? Stressed? Frustrated? Open-minded? Intrigued? Are you thinking, 'They're going to ask me for something … try to sell me something … get me to fill in a questionnaire'? Do you put on your 'It's the local eccentric! Get me out of here!' face and look the other way?

The same process may well be going through the mind of the hapless stranger you approach in a Provençal village to find out some local gen.

Theme 2	
Section 2:8	

Our courageous traveller is looking for an ATM. How does he try to put his 'victim' at ease?

> – Excusez-moi, madame!
> Oui?
> – Bonjour.
> Bonjour, monsieur.
> – C'est pour un renseignement.
> D'accord.
> – Je suis anglais. Mon français n'est pas trop bon.
> Vous parlez très bien français.
> – Merci. S'il vous plaît, je cherche un distributeur de billets.

His strategy is:

* to have an idea beforehand of what he wants to say
* to start off politely:

Excusez-moi, madame! *Excuse me!*
Bonjour. *Good morning.*

* to set the scene:

C'est pour un renseignement. *I need some information.*
Je suis anglais. *I'm English.*
Mon français n'est pas trop bon. *My French isn't too great.*

* to stick to his guns and use his prepared sentence:

Je cherche un distributeur de billets. *I'm looking for an ATM.*

* he recognises the compliment that he speaks French well – **Vous parlez très bien français** – and is able to respond:

Merci. *Thank you.*

* he also remembers to be polite:

S'il vous plaît. *Please.*

So far, so good; he has got his message across. The next challenge is going to be understanding the reply! Or to ask further questions to clarify it if not. (More of that in Theme 4.) You can listen to the conversation on the DVD, with or without looking at the written version. Some people like seeing things written down; others find it distracting, as they get confused between the spelling and the pronunciation. You'll eventually discover the mix of listening, reading and speaking that works best for you. Try to say the words aloud, and adapt the conversation so that it works for you.

The big differences

AGREEMENT

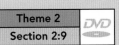

Theme 2	
Section 2:9	

Français (French) is the word for both the language and the nationality. To make it clear whether you are talking about a French man or a French woman, the word changes slightly in both the way it's written and the way it's said. So, if a man is French, he would say **Je suis français** (the final **s** is silent), while a Frenchwoman would say **Je suis française** (the extra **e** means you pronounce the **s**).

TRY IT OUT

Armed with this information, how would you change:

Je suis anglais (I am English – male) if you're female?

Je suis écossais (I am Scottish – male) if you're female?

Je suis gallois (I am Welsh – male) if you're female?

Je suis irlandais (I am Irish – male) if you're female?

If you're **britannique** (British) it looks and sounds the same for women and men. You can hear the male and female forms of these nationalities on your DVD.

For more on gender and adjectives see Toolkit, pages 118-119

Pause for thought

French people you come across may react in any number of ways. Some will rigorously correct your accent and grammar, others will simply not make any allowances for you, or try to understand, unless what you say is pretty good. You need to be patient and remember that:

- you almost certainly won't understand everything people say
- you probably won't be able to respond very quickly
- you probably won't pick up on the regional accents easily
- you may be confused by some behaviour (e.g. what we call the 'Gallic shrug').

It's often up to you to take the initiative, give your best, keep the conversation on track and get on people's right side. Don't underestimate the importance of eye contact, body language and confidence – this counts almost as much as the words themselves.

Theme 2	
Section 1:3	

Throughout the programmes, you see how Marcus' comedy performance improves as he gets more into character. Ultimately, it is his physical acting that brings a smile to people's faces. Watch this video clip, and see how he has also carefully observed the French around him, so that he's able to make jokes relevant to his audience – focusing on the southern accent, sending himself up as 'not bad for an Englishman', referring to the Olympic Games controversy – basically attempting to see things from their perspective.

Making new language

Our hero was looking for **un distributeur de billets** *(an ATM)*. You could probably have worked out what the phrase meant by literally translating the French – a 'distributor of banknotes'. He used the expression **Je cherche** *(I'm looking for)*, which will come in handy in many other situations when you're looking for a specific place. If you're with someone else, you can adjust it to **On cherche** *(We're looking for)*.

Look at the Language Wheel below, and try saying all the sentences. You can hear them on the DVD. Note that **Je cherche** on its own means *'I am looking for'* (i.e. there is no need to use a separate word for 'for'). Again, think about creating a memory hook, mental or visual, to help you remember new bits of French. For **chercher** *(to look for)* you might, for instance, have a picture in mind of a detective searching for a church (because of the vague similarity between **cherche** and 'church'). You could also remember it by noting that **cherche** is a bit like the English 'search'. People remember things in different ways, so find a method that best suits you.

Theme 2	DVD
Section 2:10	

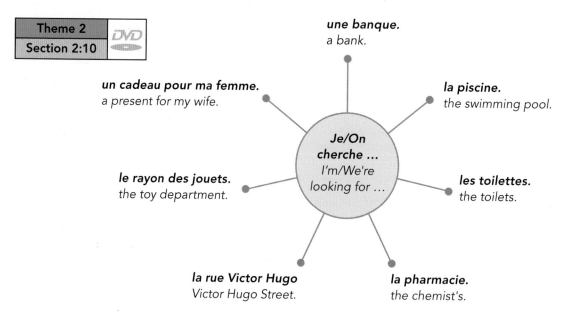

une banque.
a bank.

un cadeau pour ma femme.
a present for my wife.

la piscine.
the swimming pool.

Je/On cherche ...
I'm/We're looking for ...

le rayon des jouets.
the toy department.

les toilettes.
the toilets.

la rue Victor Hugo
Victor Hugo Street.

la pharmacie.
the chemist's.

TRY IT OUT

Theme 2	DVD
Section 2:11	

Make a Language Wheel for yourself of things you might want to say, starting with **Je cherche ...** *(I'm looking for ...)*. Keep an open mind. You could use this to ask the way somewhere, if you're trying to find a specific item in a supermarket or department store, to find out where something is in a hotel – or in many other situations.

To get you started, in a hotel, how could you say you're looking for:

1 the lift?

2 the way out?

3 a telephone?

4 your room?

Suggested answers are at the back of the book, and you can also hear them on your DVD.

l'ascenseur *lift*

la chambre *room*

la sortie *way out*

The big differences

ON

On is used a great deal in day-to-day French to mean 'you' or 'we' in a general sense.

On y va? *Shall we go?*
On prend la voiture? *Shall we take the car?*
On est prêt? *Are we (all) ready?*

It's a bit like the English 'one', but one doesn't use this very much any more, does one? ***On*** doesn't carry the same stigma of sounding posh or old-fashioned in French, and you'll hear it used instead of ***nous*** *(we)* a lot.

The main parts of the verb you'll meet in this book are those that are most commonly used in spoken French. While you may want to learn all six parts of French verbs, you'll mainly use just three of them, shown in bold below. Listen to how these are said on your DVD.

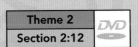

Theme 2	
Section 2:12	

For more on verbs see Toolkit, page 121

chercher to look for		
je (I)	**cherche**	I am looking for
tu (you – *informal*)	cherch**es**	you are looking for
il/elle/**on** (he/she/we, you)	**cherche**	he/she is/We are looking for
nous (we)	cherch**ons**	we are looking for
vous (you – *formal or plural*)	**cherchez**	you are looking for
ils/elles (they)	cherch**ent**	they are looking for

BEING PREPARED

It helps to think in advance about some of the activities you might want to do in France, so that you can look up the specialist French you'll want. Write a checklist of specific questions, words and phrases you might need for your special interest, for example wine-tasting, waterskiing or photography, using a dictionary, phrasebook or on-line resource. You could set it out as a Language Map, if you like. The pronunciation guide on the DVD should help you work out how to say any new words.

As well as your special interest French, you'll want to make a note of useful and recurring language that you can recycle in all sorts of situations. Some examples of such key expressions that you've already met include:

S'il vous plaît *Please, excuse me (useful for attracting attention)*

Je cherche ... *I'm looking for ...*

Vous avez ...? *Have you got ...?*

Il y a ...? *Is there any ...? Are there any ...?*

TRY IT OUT

| Theme 2 | DVD |
| Section 2:13 | |

Using some of these phrases, how would you say the following?

1 I'm looking for the toilets, please.

2 Have you got any stamps?

3 Excuse me, is there a bank near here?

You can see suggested answers at the back of the book, and hear them on your DVD.

une banque *bank*

des timbres *some stamps*

TRY IT OUT

Reading in French can help you expand your vocabulary and remind you of things you had forgotten you knew. In an on-line message board posting, a Frenchwoman is looking for a holiday house swap. Read the message, and see which bits of French would be useful to you. Look out for:

1 details of the writer's family and where they live

2 what sort of exchange they are looking for

3 what their home is like.

You can see answers and a translation of the posting at the back of the book.

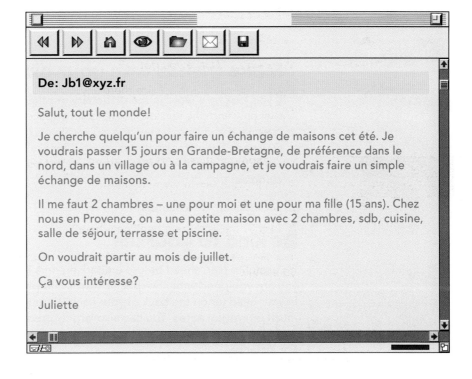

De: Jb1@xyz.fr

Salut, tout le monde!

Je cherche quelqu'un pour faire un échange de maisons cet été. Je voudrais passer 15 jours en Grande-Bretagne, de préférence dans le nord, dans un village ou à la campagne, et je voudrais faire un simple échange de maisons.

Il me faut 2 chambres – une pour moi et une pour ma fille (15 ans). Chez nous en Provence, on a une petite maison avec 2 chambres, sdb, cuisine, salle de séjour, terrasse et piscine.

On voudrait partir au mois de juillet.

Ça vous intéresse?

Juliette

salut *hi*

tout le monde *everybody*

quelqu'un *somebody*

je voudrais *I'd like*

le jour *day*

à la campagne in the country

la chambre bedroom

chez nous at (our) home

partir to set off/go away

juillet July

sdb (la salle de bains) bathroom

un an year

Make friends with your dictionary

If you look up a word in the dictionary or other reference work, you may well only find one version given, to save space. This will typically be the masculine and singular version, so you'll need to adapt it to the form you want. For instance, if looking up 'Chinese' you'll find *chinois*. If you want to talk about a Chinese girl or woman you'll have to change it to *chinoise*.

Be kind to yourself

It's useful to plan ahead before embarking on a French conversation, so that you are equipped with any specific words and phrases you need. This can be in your head (or on the back of your hand) though it's best not to rely too much on written notes. You can also largely predict the sort of answer you are hoping to receive, so run through these in your mind before you start. For instance:

- if you are asking about prices you're likely to hear numbers in the reply
- if you are asking about timetables you're likely to hear times
- if you are asking for a cashpoint, you're likely to hear directions.

Even if the answer you get includes other things, it's unlikely you'll need to translate it all – you're just on the lookout for a specific detail. When you spot this detail, repeat it back to the person to confirm you've got it right, perhaps using **hein?**.

Theme 2	
Section 1:4	

In this video clip watch Marcus talking about his journey to Saint-Tropez. You don't need to understand every single word; from his gestures and tone you can work out whether he has enjoyed the trip or not. Watching without subtitles will help train your eye and ear.

Theme 2	
Section 4	

DVD Challenge

Time for an interactive challenge on the DVD! Take part in a conversation with a Frenchman in a busy bar. Follow the prompts on screen to play your part. You can see the transcripts and the translations at the back of the book.

DO

- try to create personalised visual or mental 'memory hooks' to help learn new terms
- think ahead when asking questions, and prepare yourself for possible responses

DON'T

- forget to say hello to passers-by and shopkeepers
- be let down by your pronunciation. Listen to how the French say it, copy them and practise, practise, practise

3

Getting what you want

This Theme explores some ways of getting what you want out of situations when shopping, at outdoor markets or on the high street. Being able to ask about specific items, or talk about your size and personal taste, will mean you're more likely to come out with the item you went in for, or something you actually like!

CHALLENGE – SO, WHAT DO YOU WANT TO DO?

Some of the challenges you might pick for yourself are to:

- recognise names of shops
- ask if there is (a chemist's or other place) nearby
- name some common shopping items
- ask where an item is
- ask for something by weight or quantity
- ask to try something (on)
- check and understand prices

and there may well be others, more personal or quirky.

When you're in France, you'll sometimes want to try the local food and drink (*les spécialités*) – down in Provence you could experience the local melons, olives, cheeses, fruit and vegetables, cakes and sweets, or, on the coast, oysters, seafood or the famous fish stew *bouillabaisse*, a speciality of Marseille. Not to mention the wine or sampling a glass (or several) of pastis!

But, in addition to all those new flavours, there are some staple foods you may be asking for at the market or the corner shop, according to your own tastes and eating habits. Listen to this dialogue on your DVD, between a woman and the owner of a fruit and vegetable stall. Make a note of the different ways she says what she wants.

Theme 3	DVD
Section 2:1	

— Bonjour, monsieur.
  Bonjour. Qu'est-ce qu'il vous faut?
— Je voudrais des melons. Je peux ...?
  Allez-y, je vous en prie. Ils sont bien mûrs. Deux euros la pièce.
— D'accord. Il m'en faut deux, s'il vous plaît ... et des cerises – je peux goûter?
  Bien sûr.
— Oui. Je vais en prendre un kilo.
  Ce sera tout?
— Oui, merci. Ça fait combien?
  Sept euros cinquante, s'il vous plaît.

— Good morning.
  Morning. What can I do for you? (What do you need?)
— I'd like some melons. May I ...? (Here, this indicates that you might want to pick one up, smell it, feel how ripe it is, etc.)
  Please go ahead. They're (nice and) ripe. €2 each.
— OK. I need two please ... and some cherries. May I taste?
  Of course.
— Yes, I'll have (take) a kilo.
  Will that be all?
— Yes thanks. How much is that?
  €7.50 please.

Je voudrais (*I would like*) deserves a special mention, as it's one of the hardest-worked phrases in the language. Use it to ask for things in a shop or to order in a restaurant. *Il me faut ...* (*I need ...*) is also very useful. You can use it to start a list of things you want. *Je vais prendre ...* (*I'll have/I'll take ...*) comes in handy when you've made a decision and are saying what you are going to buy. You can use it in:

* a café – *Je vais prendre une eau minérale* (*I'll have a mineral water*)
* a shop – *Je vais en prendre cent (100) grammes* (*I'll take 100g of it/them*)
* a restaurant – *Je vais prendre le plat du jour* (*I'll have the dish of the day*)

and that's just for starters!

Theme 3	
Section 2:2	*DVD*

TRY IT OUT

Write a shopping list of things you buy regularly, starting with **Il me faut ...** *(I need ...)*. Use a dictionary or phrasebook to find the French words, or look at the labels on items in the cupboards or fridge in your kitchen – they often include French. To get you started, listen to this audio clip on your DVD. You'll hear people asking for various items – match what you hear with the pictures below. If you might want to buy the same things, practise saying them aloud (you'll find the transcripts at the back of the book if you want to see or note down the spellings, as well as the translations). Even if you don't like all these items and won't be buying some of them, it's still good to be able to recognise them when you hear them. That way you can say no if someone offers you some!

A

B

C

D

E

F

40

GET STUCK IN

When you've written your list of desirable foodstuffs, you'll want to find a way of memorising them. After all, you don't want to be carrying sheaves of papers around to the grocer's with you every day. If these are things you've already got at home, you could borrow Marcus' strategy of using sticky labels. Write the names in French onto labels and place them on the cupboard, fridge, shelf, jar, pot or container where you keep that item. That way, every time you go to get it, you'll see the word in French. If you then say it aloud it will help cement it in your memory even more firmly.

The big differences

SINGULAR AND PLURAL

When trying to speak a new language, people are often wary of saying anything at all for fear of getting the details wrong. Some details clearly are important as, if you get them wrong, you might be incomprehensible. However, as we learn from Ron's example, being unintelligible is not necessarily an obstacle to successful communication!

A lot of the details people worry about are only really obvious in the written language, and lapses and errors in speech can be overlooked in the flow of things. Singular and plural forms are in this category. They're usually not critical to worry about, as people will be able to tell from the context what you're talking about, but it's still worth knowing a bit about them, as so many words are affected.

In English you can see and hear the difference, even if not all words follow the same pattern:

a melon – melons
the carrot – the carrots
a woman – women
the mouse – the mice

The plural form in English can usually be heard by the '-s' on the end. In French, you see the difference rather than hear it (as the final **-s** is silent). Instead, the plural is heard in the word that comes before: **des** (some); **les** (the); **mes** (my) etc.

<u>un</u> **melon** – <u>des</u> **melons** a melon – some melons
<u>une</u> **carotte** – <u>des</u> **carottes** a carrot – some carrots
<u>le</u> **melon** – <u>les</u> **melons** the melon – the melons
<u>la</u> **carotte** – <u>les</u> **carottes** the carrot – the carrots

For more on singular and plural see Toolkit, page 119

MORE SHOPPING

Theme 3	
Section 2:3	

If you can get away from the **spécialités**, markets sell more than food and drink. At a clothes stall you might need to make choices regarding size and colour for a holiday gift to take home. In this conversation look out for how the customer a) makes her choice clear, b) expresses opinions and c) checks the price.

> – S'il vous plaît, je voudrais un short pour ma petite fille.
> Bien, madame. Quelle couleur? Je les ai en blanc, en rose ou en bleu clair, à quinze euros.
> – Elle n'aime pas le rose; elle préfère le blanc, je crois.
> D'accord. Quelle taille – petite ou moyenne?
> – Moyenne, s'il vous plaît. Quinze euros, c'est ça? Très bien – je vais prendre celui-là.
>
> – Excuse me, I'd like a pair of shorts for my little girl.
> Yes, what colour? I've got them in white, pink or pale blue for €15.
> – She doesn't like pink; she prefers white, I think.
> OK. What size – small or medium?
> – Medium, please. €15, is that right? Very good – I'll take that one.

Ça is an invaluable little word meaning *'that'* or *'that thing there'*. When you don't know the name of the thing that looks so beautiful in the window, you can always point and say **ça**.

The daughter doesn't like pink: **elle n'aime pas le rose**. **Aime** comes from the verb **aimer** (*to like*), and this verb behaves exactly like **chercher** (*to look for*) which you saw in Theme 2 (page 33).

J'aime le pastis. *I like pastis.*

Je n'aime pas le vin blanc. *I don't like white wine.*

Je préfère le champagne. *I prefer champagne.*

If you don't like something, say **je n'aime pas**.

Je n'aime pas les carottes. *I don't like carrots.*

The big differences

NEGATIVE WORDS

From *elle n'aime pas le rose* (she doesn't like pink) you can work out that *je n'aime pas* means 'I don't like'.

Je n'aime pas les carottes. I don't like carrots.
Je n'aime pas parler anglais. I don't like speaking English.

You'll spot that, in French, 'not' comes in two bits: *n'* or *ne* + *pas*, with a verb in between.

TRY IT OUT

Have another look at the sentences above and work out how to make the following sentences negative (the *n'* will be *ne* if the word doesn't start with a vowel or 'h'):

| Theme 3 | DVD |
| Section 2:4 | |

Je parle espagnol. I speak Spanish.
Je sais. I know.
Je comprends. I understand.
J'aime faire les courses. I like doing the shopping.
J'aime travailler ici. I like working here.

You can see the negative sentences at the back of the book, and hear them on the DVD.

For more on negatives see Toolkit, page 125

Making your own language

As well as using *Je voudrais* and *Il me faut*, if you're looking for specific items in a shop or market you also can recycle *Je cherche* (I'm looking for) from the Language Wheel in Theme 2. It works just as well if you are looking for biscuits or beer in the supermarket as for places in town.

Excusez-moi. Je cherche les biscuits/les bières. Excuse me. I'm looking for biscuits/beers.

Look at the items in the Language Wheel on the next page. They can all follow *Je voudrais*, *Il me faut* or *Je cherche*. So now you can make twenty-one different sentences! Try saying them out loud, and remember where to put the stress. You can hear a selection on your DVD.

Theme 3	DVD
Section 2:5	

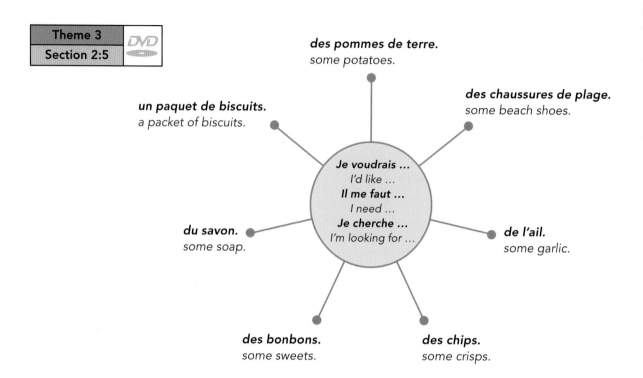

des pommes de terre.
some potatoes.

des chaussures de plage.
some beach shoes.

un paquet de biscuits.
a packet of biscuits.

Je voudrais …
I'd like …
Il me faut …
I need …
Je cherche …
I'm looking for …

du savon.
some soap.

de l'ail.
some garlic.

des bonbons.
some sweets.

des chips.
some crisps.

Theme 3	DVD
Section 3	

TRY IT OUT

Time to put into practice what you've seen so far with an interactive activity. On your DVD, listen to a conversation at a grocery shop, and work out what is being bought. You can see the transcript at the back of the book, as well as the translation.

The big differences

QUESTIONS

Shopping can involve asking a lot of questions as well as stating what you want. Remember **Vous avez ...?** (Have you got ...?) from Theme 1? This flexible phrase is useful when shopping too. As long as your voice rises towards the end of the sentence, **Vous avez** is a question – **Vous avez des timbres?** (Have you got any stamps?) or (Do you have any stamps?).

In the English, 'Do you have any stamps?', the word 'do' has no meaning of its own; it's just there to indicate a question. In French **Est-ce que ...** plays a similar role. This is easier to say than to spell, as you'll hear on the DVD! Literally it means 'Is it that ...?'. In English we might say 'Is it right/true that ...?', giving a clear signal that a question will follow.

Est-ce que vous avez des timbres? Have you got any stamps?

You'll also hear **Avez-vous ...?** It's just another way of saying the same thing.

The basic phrase **Vous avez ...?** can be adapted in a market situation, say, to ask for something more specific:

Vous l'avez en bleu? Do you have it in blue?

Vous l'avez en plus petit/grand? Do you have it in a smaller/bigger size?

You can see some examples in the Language Wheel below, and hear them on the DVD.

For more on questions see Toolkit, page 126

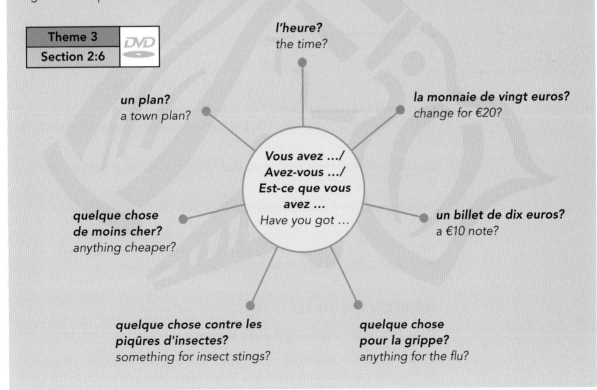

Theme 3	DVD
Section 2:6	

l'heure?
the time?

un plan?
a town plan?

la monnaie de vingt euros?
change for €20?

Vous avez .../ Avez-vous .../ Est-ce que vous avez ...
Have you got ...

quelque chose de moins cher?
anything cheaper?

un billet de dix euros?
a €10 note?

quelque chose contre les piqûres d'insectes?
something for insect stings?

quelque chose pour la grippe?
anything for the flu?

CHECKING UP

When checking on the price of shorts earlier the customer asked: **Quinze euros, c'est ça?** (€15, is that right?). **C'est** (it is) and **C'est ...?** (Is it ...?) are used in all sorts of situations. At the start of his month in Provence, Ron claims to know no French at all, but still recalls **C'est combien?** (How much is it/are they?) as an essential phrase from previous holidays!

C'est also comes at the end of the question 'What is it?', or in French, **Qu'est-ce que c'est?**. This useful question can help you out when you've forgotten a word, when you want to find out what's going on, or what the ingredients are of some fabulous dish. It is made up of:
Que (what) + **est-ce que** (marks a question)+ **c'est?** (it is/is it?)

TRY IT OUT

Theme 3	DVD
Section 2:7	

Make yourself a Language Wheel for things you might want to know the price of. Include something to eat, something to drink and an item of clothing. Here are some examples to get you started.

Une pâtisserie, c'est combien, s'il vous plaît? How much is the cake?
Les chocolats, c'est combien, s'il vous plaît? How much are the chocolates?

So, how could you ask the price of:

1 a T-shirt?

2 a bottle of mineral water?

3 melons?

You can check the answers at the back of the book, and hear them on the DVD.

C'est combien, s'il vous plaît? will stand you in good stead in whatever shop, restaurant or hotel you are, but you will hear other ways of asking the price, such as:

Ça fait combien? How much does that come to? (more often when you've bought several items)

Je vous dois combien?/Combien je vous dois? How much do I owe you?

When you get more confident you might like to bring them into your conversation for variety, but they essentially mean the same as **C'est combien?**. Different words, all leading to the same answer.

WORD ON THE STREET

Signs and notices you might want to spot

Many shops have an ending that rhymes. If you have a musical inclination, you may find memorising them as a verse helps. Listen to them on the DVD.

Theme 3	DVD
Section 2:8	

| The pork shop is | **la charcuterie** |
| And for meat that's not pork try | **la boucherie** |

For bread or for buns it's **la boulangerie**
But for fancier cakes try **la pâtisserie**

For cheeses you might see **la fromagerie**
Or for other dairy it could be **la crémerie**

A village grocer runs **l'épicerie**
While the chemist's is **la pharmacie**

As well as their *-ie* ending all of these specialist shops have something else in common – they are all feminine (**une** or **la**).

Making new language

Theme 3	DVD
Section 2:9	

Ron is constantly berated by his teacher for not using verbs. Knowing the French for individual things is all very well, but to say what you want to do with these things, you really need a verb. One of the most useful verb forms is **Je peux ...?** *(May I ...?/Can I ...?)*. This handy phrase can be used to start loads of sentences. Make some from the Language Wheel below. You can also hear them on your DVD.

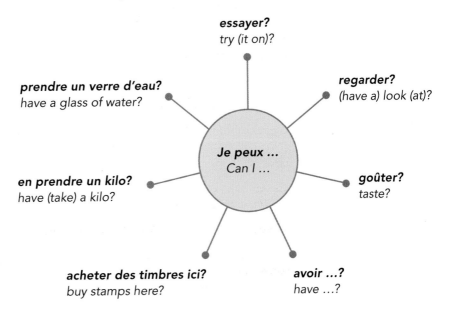

As well as using **Je peux** in sentences like these, you can pull it out of the hat on its own. Accompanied by a meaningful gesture or mime, such as holding your camera up, or pointing to a free seat, a simple **Je peux?** should also convey your question.

Make friends with your dictionary

Je peux? (*Can I?/May I?*) is a useful piece of language but you probably won't find it if you look it up in the French side of your dictionary. You probably wouldn't find 'May I …?' in an English dictionary either.

That's because they are only parts (even if very useful parts) of the whole verb they come from. In English 'May I?' or 'Can I?' is part of the verb 'to be allowed to', 'to be able to'. In French *Je peux* is part of the verb *pouvoir* (where we get the English word 'power' from). *Pouvoir* means 'to be allowed to', 'to be able to'.

You don't necessarily need to know this stuff, but it's useful when you come to look something up. If you can't find it in the dictionary you could ask yourself 'Which verb does this part come from?'. Your answer will be a word with 'to' in front of it in English, and that's the word to look up. In French there is no equivalent word for 'to', and the part of the verb that you find in a dictionary (known as the infinitive) has a particular ending, often *-er*, *-re* or *-ir*.

So, if you want to say, in English:

'I am going' → it comes from the verb 'to go' → look up 'go' in the dictionary → find *aller*
'he went' → it also comes from the verb 'to go' → look up 'go' in the dictionary → find *aller*
'they told me' > it comes from the verb 'to tell' → look up 'tell' in the dictionary → find *dire*
'I am' → it comes from the verb 'to be' → look up 'be' in the dictionary → find *être*

TRY IT OUT

Which English verbs do these parts come from? And can you find the French verbs as well?

1 I am reading

2 She was watching

3 Will we need?

4 I thought

5 Did you say?

6 Are they coming?

7 What is she doing?

You can see the answers at the back of the book.

This is just the first step to making up exactly what you want to say. You'll still need to work out the right form of the verb in French, but at least you'll be on the right track.

TRY IT OUT

Theme 3	*DVD*
Section 2:10	

Try to work out what you could say in the following situations, using any of the expressions you've met in this Theme so far. There's no single right way to say these – you'll find a range of possible answers at the back of the book, and you can hear them on your DVD.

1 How could you get your message across to obtain a bottle of water?

2 What might you say to ask someone (on a train maybe) if you can look at their magazine?

3 How about asking if you can try on **un tee-shirt** or **des baskets** (*some trainers*)?

une bouteille d'eau *a bottle of water*

regarder *to look at*

un magazine *a magazine*

essayer *to try (on/out)*

If you're shopping for food, you will probably want to ask for different measurements or amounts of things.

By slice, or piece: **une tranche, une part, un morceau**
By weight, in: **grammes, kilos, un demi-kilo** (*half-kilo*), **une livre** (*500g*), **demi-livre** (*250g*)
Individually: **la pièce** (*each*)
By volume: **un litre, un demi-litre** (*half-litre*), **une bouteille** (*a bottle*)
By container: **une boîte** (*a box, a tin*), **un paquet** (*a packet*), **un bocal** (*a jar*)

or just by asking for 'some …'.

The big differences

SOME

What's the difference between: *Je voudrais du brie* and *Je voudrais deux cent grammes de brie*? It's about precision – the first just says '*I want some Brie*', leaving the cheesemonger at liberty to give you tonnes of the stuff if he feels like it! The second specifies precisely how much Brie you want, i.e. 200g.

The word for '*some*' changes with the word it relates to:

du brie because Brie is masculine (*le brie*), as is cheese in general (*le fromage*),
de l'eau (*some water*) because *eau* starts with a vowel,
de la limonade (*some lemonade*) because it is feminine (*la limonade*), and
des oignons (*some onions*) because it's plural. You'll need these later on.

Note that *de + le = du* and *de + les = des*.

By itself the word *de* means 'of' or 'from': *une bouteille d'eau* (a bottle of water).

You'll meet more words like this (prepositions) in Theme 4.

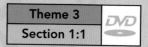

Theme 3	
Section 1:1	*DVD*

Watch this clip of Marcus food shopping at the market. His mission is to buy some fish (a type called *la lotte*) and a mystery item – *deux grenades*. How might he ask for these things politely and which of the words for 'some' might he choose? Suggested answers at the back of the book.

For more on prepositions see Toolkit, page 120

Be kind to yourself

Planning is of the essence! Learning to use a language takes lots of confidence, practice and effort, so you don't want to be using up what time you have with pointless tasks. Reading and writing words can be helpful, but in some situations you're more likely to want to understand and use the spoken word.

For example, for most people there is no real purpose in knowing how to spell numbers in words. In real life we write numbers as figures – 13 or 76 rather than 'thirteen' or 'seventy six' (*treize, soixante-seize*.) For this reason, when learning numbers, focus on practising how to recognise the number quickly when you hear it. You may also want to practise saying numbers out loud.

A lot of the time when people are talking French around you, all you need is the general sense of what is going on, and a good eye and ear to notice the clues:

- the tone of voice
- the things they are pointing at
- the facial expressions.

Understanding numbers is one of the occasions when it is important to grasp the detail of what you hear, as a mistake made over a price or a phone number could prove costly or embarrassing.

NUMBERS IN PRICES

Theme 3	DVD
Section 2:11	

The range of numbers you need to know depends, of course, on the amounts you tend to spend! For everyday shopping at a street market or café the range is limited. (There'll be bigger numbers for travellers who buy lots of Lamborghinis!)

Prices are in euros, so first you need to recognise how a French person says the word *euro*. Listen to the clip on your DVD to get used to the sound of these prices.

un (1) euro

quatre (4) euros

cinq (5) euros

sept (7) euros

huit (8) euros

Theme 3	DVD
Section 2:12	

You can also hear how the numbers 1-10 sound. Remember that the written words may confuse you – try just listening to them so you're not tempted to pronounce them with an English accent. If you want to see the words written though, here they are:

1 un	6 six
2 deux	7 sept
3 trois	8 huit
4 quatre	9 neuf
5 cinq	10 dix

The 'teen' numbers are the ones that tend to catch people out; you need to be sure you are clear about the differences between the 'teen' numbers (e.g. **quatorze**, fourteen) and the 'ten' numbers (e.g. **quarante**, forty).

The tougher ones are:

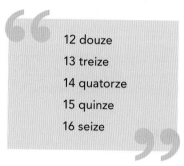

12 douze

13 treize

14 quatorze

15 quinze

16 seize

And then the more 'logical' ones:

17 dix-sept

18 dix-huit

19 dix-neuf

So you can really go to town with these basic numbers in your head, give them a good workout. First try saying the number in the gap on the audio clip, and then play it again and say the numbers at the same time as the voice.

Theme 3	
Section 2:13	

All of these numbers are used to make prices, but some sound different when followed by the **eu** sound of **euros**. You might notice that you hear an extra sound on the end of these numbers (to smooth the way into the '**e**' of **euro**) – if you look this up in a reference book, it's called 'liaison'. Generally, if a word ends in a consonant, you don't sound it, but if the following word begins with a vowel, these words run together and you do sound it.

2€ (deux euros)

3€ (trois euros)

13€ (treize euros)

6€ (six euros)

9€ (neuf euros)

19€ (dix-neuf euros)

Theme 3	DVD
Section 2:14	

Many prices including *centimes*, euro cents, are rounded to the nearest ten, so you might also hear some of these 'ten' numbers tagged on at the end of a price. These numbers are also pronounced on your DVD.

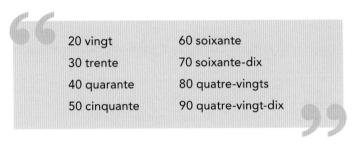

> 20 vingt   60 soixante
>
> 30 trente   70 soixante-dix
>
> 40 quarante   80 quatre-vingts
>
> 50 cinquante   90 quatre-vingt-dix

You can combine these with the smaller numbers you've already met, to make other numbers. For instance: *vingt-cinq* (25), *quarante-huit* (48).

In real life, people don't necessarily do what we'd like them to and speak in full sentences. Just as we'd say 'one fifty' as shorthand for 'one pound and fifty pence', the French will often abbreviate prices, and say just *un cinquante* ('one fifty', meaning 'one euro fifty centimes').

TRY IT OUT

Theme 3	DVD
Section 2:15	

Here's some more practice with prices. Before you listen to the DVD, think how these prices would be said. They are said in a different order on the DVD – as you hear each one, mark the order by writing a number in the box beside it. You can see the correct order at the back of the book.

€1.20 ☐   €18.10 ☐

€1.80 ☐   €4.90 ☐

€5.50 ☐   €8.70 ☐

€20 ☐   €6.75 ☐

Theme 3	DVD
Section 1:2	

Now watch this video clip of Esther trying to buy a ticket at the train station, and see if you can identify:

1 the age range for qualifying for the ticket

2 how old Esther says she is

3 and for a bonus point, the times the ticket clerk mentions (in the 24-hour clock).

You can see the answers, as well as a transcript and translation, at the back of the book.

Pause for thought

When planning what to say to someone, try to decide what they need to know, and anticipate what they might ask. Being prepared and flexible will stand you in good stead if the conversation doesn't follow a textbook example. A textbook dialogue, of someone buying an ice-cream from a stand, might go:

Theme 2
Section 2:16

> – Bonjour.
> Bonjour, mademoiselle.
> – Je voudrais une glace.
> Oui. Quel parfum?
> – Chocolat, s'il vous plaît.
> Voilà. Ça fait un euro cinquante.
>
> – Good morning.
> Good morning.
> – I'd like an ice-cream.
> Yes. What flavour?
> – Chocolate, please.
> There you are. That'll be €1.50.

Sympathise with the poor traveller who, equipped with this expectation, has the following experience with an impatient ice-cream seller:

> – Bonjour.
> Bonjour, mademoiselle.
> – Je voudrais une glace.
> Oui. Vous êtes au bon endroit. Combien de boules?
> – Euh … Comment?
> Combien de boules? *(waving the ice-cream scoop)*
> – Ah … chocolat, s'il vous plaît.
> Oui, d'accord, mais combien de boules?
> – Euh … *(I've no idea what he's saying!)*

Exit noble traveller, crestfallen and **sans** *(without)* ice-cream.

54

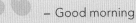

> – Good morning.
>   Good morning.
> – I'd like an ice-cream.
>   Yes. You're in the right place. How many scoops?
> – Erm … Sorry? (Pardon)
>   How many scoops?
> – Ah … chocolate, please.
>   Yes, OK, but how many scoops?
> – Erm …

You can hear the first dialogue on the DVD. In the second dialogue, the intrepid ice-cream seeker's first problem is a deviation from the 'script'. When she asks for an ice-cream, she gets a sarcastic response: **Oui. Vous êtes au bon endroit.** She's talking to someone whose job is to sell ice-cream; all he has in front of him is tubs of the stuff. Is it really necessary to bother saying 'I'd like an ice-cream'?

The second problem is that the question she hears is not the one she had prepared. Instead of 'What flavour?' she gets **Combien de boules?**. 'How many scoops?' is, in a way, quite a predictable enquiry, as the seller is keen to sell as much ice cream as possible.

The third problem is that she doesn't get what she wanted – an ice-cream!

In terms of strategy, she does try to get back into the conversation with a well-chosen word to show she is thinking **Euh …** (Erm …) and asks him to repeat the question: **Comment?** (Pardon?). Unfortunately she misinterprets the waving scoop as meaning 'Which one?' and simply asks for a particular flavour: **Chocolat, s'il vous plaît.**

So, what other strategies could she have tried? Being more assertive is one. She needed to be more assertive in order to make sure she got what she wanted. Her options now are to:

* repeat her mantra of **chocolat** and pointing until he is worn down
* check what his question means by saying it back to him, while showing she hasn't understand, through intonation, facial expression, or body language
* make a direct request for help: **Combien de boules? Je ne comprends pas.** (How many scoops? I don't understand). Or **Qu'est-ce que c'est, 'combien de boules?'** (What does 'how many scoops' mean?). He might then relent and make his question clearer, by rephrasing, or demonstrating what the scoop is for!

Theme 3	DVD
Section 1:3	

Out of the celebrities on the DVD, Ron clearly has most difficulty in remembering his French and getting it out correctly (especially in sentences). However, he is able to communicate with people effectively, and be part of the fun in social situations. He has particular difficulty (as would we all) when he has no live audience to interact with, for example on the radio, because his skills are very much based on his body language, perseverance and personality. In real life encounters, however, Ron's skills are often fit for the purpose he needs them for. His objectives may just be:

- to meet the football team
- to find out their names
- to show them what they're doing well and not so well
- to socialise.

in which case – job done. Watch this video clip of Ron's half-time talk, and see how he manages to get his message across, in spite of his limited French.

MARCEL'S ONION SOUP

Have a look at this genuine recipe for a delicious onion soup. It may look completely indecipherable, but if you break it down in a systematic way, you'll soon be able to make sense of it.

Pour faire une soupe à l'oignon pour cinq personnes

un kilo d'oignons

un peu de beurre ou d'huile

farine (deux cuillères à soupe)

vin blanc sec (un demi-litre)

bouillon de poulet ou bœuf (deux litres)

sel et poivre

pain sec (une baguette)

250g de fromage râpé (gruyère de préférence)

- faites revenir les oignons dans le beurre (ou l'huile) jusqu'à ce qu'ils soient juste dorés

- mixez

- ajoutez la farine et mélangez

- remuez lentement avec le vin blanc, à feu doux (salez et poivrez si nécessaire)

- faites deux litres de bouillon et mélangez avec les oignons, chauffez doucement pendant une demi-heure – c'est la partie liquide de la soupe

- coupez le pain en fines tranches et grillez légèrement

- prenez un plat creux, et mettez au fond une couche de pain grillé, suivi d'une couche de gruyère

- versez du liquide dessus, juste pour mouiller

- ajoutez une deuxième couche de pain grillé, suivi d'une couche de gruyère, et versez encore du liquide dessus pour mouiller

- mettez au four pour faire griller le dessus – c'est la partie 'croûtons' de la soupe

- pour servir la soupe, on met dans l'assiette une part de croûtons avec une part de liquide par-dessus

Your first step in deciphering this recipe should be to think about what you already know about cooking. What are the sorts of words you typically find in any recipe? For instance, there could be instructions (these often end with *-ez* in French, like the *vous* parts of verbs), timings, names of utensils, staple ingredients. Do you know any of these words in French already?

Next, look at the ingredients list: which ones do you recognise? Clearly one essential ingredient will be onions! You met this word earlier in this Theme. Do you remember it? Which words do you not recognise at all? They may need to be looked up in a moment, but first try to work them out through a process of elimination.

Glance through the steps of the recipe, putting together what you've already discovered or thought about. Does it start to make some sort of sense? If you know, for instance, that *farine* is 'flour', what instruction could *mélangez* possibly be? There are only so many things you can do with flour!

Now, there will still be some words left that strike you as being important and that you don't know, so you can look those up in your dictionary, phrasebook or on-line.

Finally, you should be able to go through the steps one-by-one, giving a rough interpretation of what it is you are supposed to do. The best test for your reading here would be to make the onion soup yourself. It is *délicieux* (*delicious*)! You can also see a full translation at the back of the book.

Make friends with your dictionary

You can probably see straight away what these potential purchases are:

enveloppes
cartes
souvenirs
magazines

And if you heard them spoken, you should be able to recognise them too (remembering to expect the stress on the last syllable).

Not all words that look and sound similar mean the same in French and English. There are some instances where the meanings of words used to have more in common, but have drifted apart over the ages (just as our history and politics have done). These are sometimes called 'false friends', words you think you recognise but actually have a slightly or completely different meaning.

So, if you get a strange response because you've used a word you thought sounded OK, it's worth checking in the dictionary!

la monnaie is not 'money', but *'change'* ('money' is **argent**)
la pièce is not 'a piece', but *'a coin'* (also *'a room'*, and also the word for *'each'* in a shop, e.g. **le camembert, deux euros la pièce**, Camembert, €2 each)
l'essence is not 'essence' or 'perfume', but *'petrol'*
location is not 'location' but *'a hire agency'* (usually car hire)
chips are actually *'crisps'* ('chips' are **frites**)
la librairie is a *'bookshop'* (as opposed to *'library'*, which is **bibliothèque**)
la serviette can be what it looks like, but is usually *'a towel'*
les préservatifs are not preservatives, but *'condoms'* – do avoid asking someone selling jam if it contains preservatives!

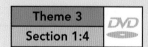

Theme 3	
Section 1:4	

Watch this video clip of Thierry talking to Esther, and make a note of all the words which sound similar in French and English, and check whether they are **faux amis** *(false friends)*. You can see the answers at the back of the book.

Theme 3	
Section 4	

DVD Challenge

Time for an interactive challenge. Take part in this conversation with the owner of a clothes stall at a market. Follow the prompts on screen to play your part. You can see the transcripts, as well as the translations, at the back of your book.

DO

- recycle the French you've learnt from one situation to another

- be prepared to listen for details you need to understand

- make sure you know basic words like numbers

- brainstorm in advance what words and questions might come up in different shops

DON'T

- bother learning how to spell words you only need to say or listen out for

- be surprised if the conversation doesn't proceed according to script

- think you have to understand every single word you hear

4

Getting around

WHAT DO YOU WANT TO DO?

When travelling around France, by whatever means of transport you choose, some of the challenges you might set yourself are to:

- ask or check the way
- understand directions
- check distances
- say place names ... and recognise them when you hear them!
- make a train/coach/bus booking
- check times and departure points
- ask for special requirements
- understand signs on the road, or at the station/airport/bus station
- buy fuel (this doesn't usually require any language nowadays, beyond checking the price)
- park safely

As ever, there will be specific things you will want to do to fit in with your own travel arrangements and interests; you may need specialist language for bike hire or motorcycle parts, or words related to footwear and foot-care if you'll be doing lots of long-distance walking. You'll need to create a personalised Language Map for that. (You'll find some sources to help you with this on page six.)

ASKING THE WAY

<table>
<tr><td>Theme 4</td><td rowspan="2">DVD</td></tr>
<tr><td>Section 2:1</td></tr>
</table>

You can ask for directions in several ways. In Theme 2 you met **Il y a … près d'ici?** *(Is there … near here?)* and **Je cherche** *(I'm looking for)*, which can both be used to ask questions. Picture the scene as a theatre-goer arrives in town, late for a play. Depending on how anxious he is, he might say:

Où se trouve le théâtre, s'il vous plaît? *Where is the theatre situated, please?*
Pour le théâtre, s'il vous plaît. *The theatre, please.*
Pour aller au théâtre, s'il vous plaît? *How do I get to the theatre, please?*
S'il vous plaît, le théâtre? *Please, the theatre?*
Or just: **Le théâtre?** *The theatre?* (with an 'I'm so late!' expression).

You can hear all these phrases on your DVD.

<table>
<tr><td>Theme 4</td><td rowspan="2">DVD</td></tr>
<tr><td>Section 2:2</td></tr>
</table>

Here are some other ways of getting help with directions – also on the DVD. Note down the pieces of language that could be useful in other situations, especially the ones you like the look or sound of, or find easy to remember.

> S'il vous plaît!
> C'est pour un renseignement.
> On cherche le marché.
> Excuse me (please)!
> I need some information.
> We're looking for the market.
>
> Excusez-moi!
> Je voudrais un renseignement.
> Il y a une station-service près d'ici, s'il vous plaît?
> Excuse me!
> I need (am looking for) some information.
> Is there a petrol station nearby, please?
>
> Monsieur!
> J'ai besoin d'un renseignement.
> Savez-vous où je peux acheter des timbres?
> Excuse me! *(to a man)*
> I need some information.
> Do you know where I can buy stamps?
>
> Madame!
> Je suis désolé de vous déranger. Vous êtes d'ici?
> Je suis étranger et je ne trouve pas l'office du tourisme.
> Excuse me! *(to a woman)*
> Sorry to bother you. Are you from around here?
> I'm a stranger (foreigner) and I can't find the tourist office.

61

Theme 4
Section 2:3

TRY IT OUT

How could you use some of these expressions to ask the way:

1 to the petrol station?

2 to the town hall square?

3 to the car park?

4 to Grenoble Street?

There is no single correct way to ask each question – you can see a range of suggested answers at the back of the book, and hear them on the DVD.

la place square

la mairie town hall

le parking car park

la rue street

ON THE ROAD

A street could be called a variety of things, depending on the size of the place you are visiting. Here it is **une rue**, but it could also be:

une avenue (tree-lined avenue)
un boulevard (street in larger towns and cities)
une allée (tree-lined walk, or major avenue)
un passage (tends to be a smaller street)
un cours (seen in Provence; often an elegant 19th-century street)
une rocade (chic name for ring-road)
une corniche (also chic, a coastal road)
une route (the road from one place to another; **la route de Gordes** is the road that goes to Gordes. **Route** is otherwise what's called a false friend, not meaning exactly the same as the English word 'route', **l'itinéraire** in French.

There are also **les places** (squares), and if you're in **une impasse** there will be only one way out! Although **cul-de-sac** was originally borrowed from French, it's not used much for the kind of streets we refer to by that name in English; it's used more to indicate a dead end.

Be kind to yourself

USE WHAT'S AROUND YOU

Being surrounded by French in an immersive experience means you are hearing new bits of language all the time, probably far too much to take in all at once. There will always be some expressions that strike you as sounding good or being especially useful, and you should make a point of reinforcing these particular phrases. You could do this by repeating them to check you've heard them right, perhaps with a little extra comment, and then trying to use them for yourself. Expanding your own bank of resources by stealing from the conversation around you is no crime!

The same is true about written words you see around you in everyday life. Once you start to surround yourself with French, you quickly start to recognise, and sometimes pick up and use, quite high-level words just because you see them a lot. Indeed, if there are things you seem to see all of the time that you can't work out from the clues around them, it's well worth asking someone what they mean – they might be important! You can use **Qu'est-ce que c'est?** (*What is it?*) to start your question.

On arrival at the airport, station or port, you may well need to recognise which of the public toilet signs is which, and store away the information for future reference. Inside the toilet you'll want to check whether the flush is one where you

MESSIEURS

DAMES

have to **tirer** (*pull*) or **appuyer** (*press*) and to be awake enough to remember that the hot tap will be labelled C (**chaud**) not H; the cold tap will be F (**froid**) not C. Finally, as you leave the terminal building you'll be faced with the instruction **tirer** (*pull*) or **pousser** (*push*) to get out of the door. Even in these few yards there are important pieces of language for you to collect!

WORD ON THE STREET

Signs and notices you might see or want to spot

One of the all-time favourite traffic signs in France has to be **Toutes directions** (*All directions*), indicating that wherever you happen to be going, this is the way! Its twin is **Autres directions** (*Other directions*), which is usually paired up with a sign to a major town (say Nîmes) or route (say the A7 – the north-south motorway in the Rhône valley), so it's indicating that unless you are going to Nîmes or the A7, all the other routes are this way.

Some other road signs to look out for on the road or in the street:

Sens unique *One way*

Travaux *Roadworks*

Embouteillage *Traffic jam*

Ne pas stationner *No parking*

Défense de stationner *No parking*

Sortie de voitures *Cars coming out (i.e. there's no parking here either!)*

Parking *Car park*

Déviation *Diversion*

Plan *(Town) map*

You probably don't need to know how to say these words, as they are things you see and understand by reading. Some of them might come in useful though.

TRY IT OUT

Theme 4	DVD
Section 2:4	

How would you:

1 check if a street is one way?

2 check if there are roadworks ahead?

3 ask for a town map?

4 ask if you can park here?

There are suggested answers at the back of the book, and you can hear them on the DVD.

Making new language

Excusez-moi madame. C'est pour un renseignement. *Excuse me. I need some information.*
Oui? *Yes?*
Pouvez-vous m'indiquer la route de Gordes? *Could you show me the way to Gordes?*

Pouvez-vous/Vous pouvez ...? *(Could you ...?)* is another one of those frequently-used pieces of language you can adapt to many situations. As well as using it when you're in need of help, you might want to suggest or request something. Use the Language Wheel below to make up some other requests, thinking of the different situations where this piece of French could help you out. You can hear the phrases on your DVD.

Theme 4	DVD
Section 2:5	

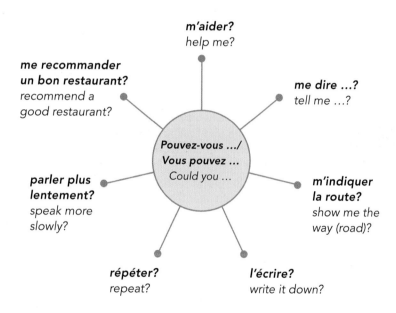

As ever, avoid translating word for word; in English we add extra words like 'down' in 'write it down' that French doesn't bother with.

TRY IT OUT

Theme 4	DVD
Section 2:6	

How might you ask someone:

1 to show you the way to Aix-en-Provence?

2 to tell you what something is?

3 to speak more slowly?

4 to recommend a restaurant?

Don't forget **s'il vous plaît** *(please)* on the end. There are suggested answers at the back of the book, and you can hear them on the DVD.

Theme 4
Section 3

DVD

GETTING IN SHAPE FOR SPEAKING

Using the alphabet

As well as **Pouvez-vous l'écrire, s'il vous plaît?** (*Could you write it down, please?*), you'll also hear the very common expression **Comment ça s'écrit?** (*How do you spell (write) it?*). You may well need to spell out a few things yourself too, and note down some words that are spelled for you. Knowing how to say the alphabet sounds like the simplest thing in the world, but if you don't think about it, it can catch you out at important moments. It's not complex to recognise and use letters in French. Bear in mind what you already know about different sounds, and use the DVD to get the pronunciation sorted.

Theme 4
Section 2:7

DVD

There are really only six letters that sound very different from their English equivalents and four of those (H, W, X, Y) are not among the most commonly used in the French language. They may however be important letters for you, if they're in your name, for instance. The letters of the alphabet fall into six groups. To help you remember them, you may want to make a Language Map. You can hear the whole alphabet on the DVD, in the following groups.

Group 1: letters whose names sound more or less as in English

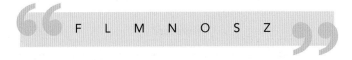

Group 2: letters whose name has the famous 'e acute' sound. (In English these rhyme, too).

Group 3: letters whose name has the French **-i** sound

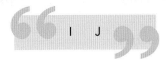

Note that G has the *-é* sound and J has the *-i* sound – the other way round to English.

Group 4: letters whose name has the French *-a* sound

A   K

Group 5: letters whose name has the French *-u* sound

Q   U

And Group 6: letters with entirely different sounding names

E   H   R   W   X   Y

E and R are very common letters, of course.

The other thing to add is that the vowels might also have accents on them; the most common are:

*é – **E accent aigu** (acute accent)*
*à – **A accent grave** (grave accent)*
*ô – **O accent circonflexe** (circumflex)*

The letter *c* can also gain a cedilla – *ç* – as in the word *français (French)* which makes it into an -s- sound.

The letter Q is ripe for mistakes and blunders, as the word *cul* (as in *cul-de-sac*) is pronounced in the same way. If you imagine that *cul-de-sac* literally means 'bottom of a bag' you can probably guess that *cul* by itself is a fairly raw word for a person's posterior. Confusion sometimes arises for people who cannot readily pronounce the difference between the French *-u-* and *-ou-* sounds. If you say *j'ai mal au cou (I've got a pain in the neck)* you may get a different response than if it is a *mal au cul* (no translation necessary!).

The *-u-* sound in French is pretty consistent, and is the sound in the word *tu*. It's not like any English sound and requires real gymnastics with the British tongue to make it feel and sound (and almost taste!) French. Try to position your mouth to say 'ooh' and then, keeping your lips and cheeks in the same position, you actually try to say 'ee'. The resulting sound is a French *-u-*.

Pause for thought

What do you want to say today? Make a checklist of things you might need to spell out for someone in French. This could include:

- spelling your family name or first name
- giving your car registration
- spelling out the name of the place you're going to
- or the place you're from
- giving a reservation code when collecting tickets.

Once you've checked how the letters should sound, work out how to spell aloud the main things on your checklist.

TRY IT OUT

Theme 4	DVD
Section 2:8	

Practise spelling these British place names aloud, letter by letter. You can hear the correct pronunciation on the DVD.

BELFAST

EDINBURGH

WREXHAM

COVENTRY

JURA

Theme 4	DVD
Section 2:9	

You'll also hear some spellings of famous places in the South of France. **Comment ça s'écrit?** (*How do you spell (write) them?*) Do you recognise them? Have a go at writing them down. You can see the correct spellings in the back of the book.

FOLLOWING DIRECTIONS

Theme 4	DVD
Section 1:1	

Asking the way is only the first part of the problem, of course. There is not a lot of point in being able to form a beautifully crafted question if you are then unable to make any sense of the reply you get! Things certainly don't go to plan when Ron is looking for somewhere good to eat. Watch this clip and work out what his problem is.

Ron had prepared in his head some of the dialogue he needed to ask his question, but not anything to help him cope with an unexpected response. A disadvantage of learning any dialogues by heart is that, in real life, people just don't follow the script! Although it doesn't work out for Ron here, he does persist and eventually finds a good restaurant. The lesson is – don't give up on what you want! You'll probably find that you'll get there after a bit of head-shaking, shrugging and saying: *Excusez-moi, je ne comprends pas* (*Excuse me, I don't understand*) and another round of: *Je cherche ...* (*I'm looking for ...*).

You can sometimes work yourself into understanding what someone is saying by picking out what seem to be the key words and repeating them back to them. Even if you don't recognise the meaning of these words, at least it shows an interest in what they're saying! It might also help to visualise (or try to write down) what those key words might look like – just the key words though, not the whole flood of French. This may give you sudden inspiration. For instance, someone giving you directions might refer to *la fontaine* (a word you don't know, but which is very common in the villages of Provence):

Vous passez devant la fontaine et puis vous tournez à gauche. *You go past the fountain and then turn left.*

You could try to picture or write just the word *fon-taine* using what you know about the French sound system. You might then make the leap to 'fountain' and be able to check by doing a mime of a fountain. The pronunciation guide in Theme 1 of the DVD (audio clips 8-14) will help you build up a sense of how sounds and spelling relate to each other in French.

One problem is that, when people give directions, they often give far too many details. To sift through this onslaught of information, there are a few steps you can take:

- before you even ask your question remind yourself of the key vocabulary you are likely to hear in the answer (see below)
- while the person is responding, pick out what you think are the key details and repeat them back, adding something like *D'accord* (*OK*) or *C'est ça?* (*Is that right?*) to show you've got it, or querying with your inflection: *La rue comment?* (*Which street?*) if you haven't
- ask them to repeat or speak more slowly: *Vous pouvez répéter? Vous pouvez parler plus lentement, s'il vous plaît?* (*Could you repeat? Could you speak more slowly, please?*)
- if you have a notebook (and every good traveller should have a notebook in their pocket!), note down or draw the key things you've understood
- at the end, check how far you think it is (time or distance) and run through the directions again (see the next page for some useful words).

WHAT ARE YOU LIKELY TO HEAR?

Theme 4	DVD
Section 2:10	

How long is a piece of string? The sort of thing you might hear depends on how big your journey is. If it's a just-around-the-corner job you may be listening for some of the words on this checklist. You can hear them on the DVD.

à gauche on/to the left

à droite on/to the right

tout droit straight on

première first

deuxième, troisième, etc. second, third, etc.

passez devant ... go past (in front of) ...

vous verrez ... you'll see ...

derrière behind

au coin at/on the corner

jusqu'à as far as

à côté de next to

en face (de) opposite

près de near to

If the nearest cash dispenser is in another village (!) you might need to add to the list:

à (cinq) kilomètres (five) kilometres away

le rond-point roundabout

les feux traffic lights

le panneau sign

marqué marked

loin far

à (dix) minutes (ten) minutes away

You might want to use **C'est loin?** *Is it far?* to check whether you can walk there or need to drive. If, like Ron, you approach someone who is not from the area, you may simply hear **Je ne suis pas d'ici** *(I'm not from around here)*.

Repeating back what's been said to you can not only keep you on the right track, but also help you feel you're part of the conversation, and gaining in confidence and fluency. Look at how the tourist does it in this conversation.

| Theme 4 | |
| Section 2:11 | |

> – S'il vous plaît. Pour aller à la Place de la République?
> Ah oui. Alors vous descendez cette avenue.
> – ... descendez cette avenue ...
> Au bout, vous prenez à gauche.
> – ... tournez à gauche?
> Oui, c'est ça. Ensuite à cent mètres de là, vous avez la place devant vous.
> – ... à cent metres de là, c'est ça?
> Voilà.
> – Merci beaucoup.
> De rien. Bonne journée.
>
> – Excuse me (please). How do I get to Place de la République?
> Ah yes. Well, you go down this street.
> – ... down this street ...
> At the end you take (the street on) the left.
> – ... turn left?
> Yes, that's it. Then, 100 metres from there, you'll see (you have) the square in front of you.
> – ... 100 metres from there – is that right?
> That's it.
> – Thank you very much.
> You're welcome. Have a good day.

You might notice that, as usual, there is more than one way of saying things. Our traveller was used to right or left being prefaced by **tournez** *(turn)*, but the informative local uses **prenez**, which literally means 'take' (the left).

TRY IT OUT

Theme 4	DVD
Section 2:12	

Using the map below, work out which of the numbered squares represent the places these three bold travellers are seeking. Start from the crossroads each time. You may prefer to listen to the directions on your DVD, without looking at the written text below. You can see answers and translations at the back of the book.

1 *Pour l'office du tourisme, vous descendez la rue de la Comédie; vous passez devant la mairie et vous tournez à droite sur la place. C'est là, à votre droite.*

2 *Pour la gare, vous prenez l'avenue Colbert. Vous allez tout droit jusqu'aux feux. Vous verrez la gare sur votre gauche.*

3 *Pour l'Hôtel St Georges, vous prenez l'avenue Colbert. Vous allez tout droit jusqu'aux feux. Vous verrez la gare sur votre gauche. Vous continuez tout droit et vous tournez encore une fois à gauche.*

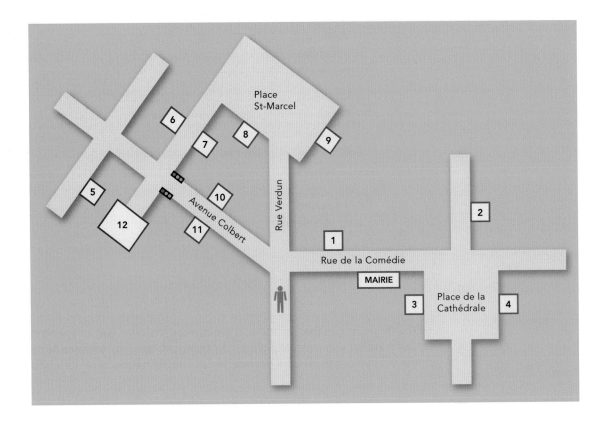

The big differences

PREPOSITIONS

You've seen that words in French have a gender – they are masculine or feminine. Whether a word takes *le* or *la* also affects words that precede it, for example, commonly-used phrases such as *jusqu'à* (as far as), *à côté de* (next to) or *près de* (near to). If you look these up in a reference book they may be listed as prepositions (prep. for short), which just means they are placed (positioned) in front of (pre-) another word. Their look and sound changes according to the gender of the words they precede.

So, 'next to the bakers' is *à côté <u>de la</u> boulangerie* (it's <u>la</u> *boulangerie*).

'Next to the bus stop' is *à côté <u>de l'</u>arrêt de bus* (because *arrêt* starts with a vowel).

But 'Next to the tobacconist's' is *à côté <u>du</u> tabac* (it's <u>le</u> *tabac*, and *de + le = du*).

'As far as the square' is *jusqu'<u>à la</u> place* (it's <u>la</u> *place*).

But 'as far as the shop' is *jusqu'<u>au</u> magasin* (it's <u>le</u> *magasin*, and *à + le = au*).

The same applies with the word 'to':

'I am going to Marseille' is *Je vais <u>à</u> Marseille* (as *Marseille* has no *le*).

'How do I get to the station?' is *Pour aller <u>à la</u> gare?*, while 'How do I get to the car park', which is masculine, is *Pour aller <u>au</u> parking?*.

Don't worry too much about getting this wrong. You'll probably still be understood, but getting the gender and preposition correct will improve the overall sound of your French.

TRY IT OUT

To practise, ask how you get to the places below using *Pour aller* followed by *à, à la, à l'* or *au*.

1 the petrol station

2 the market

3 the tourist office

4 the restaurant Chez Nico

5 Miramas

6 the baker's

You can see the answers at the back of the book, and hear them on the DVD.

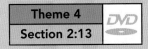

Theme 4	DVD
Section 2:13	

For more on prepositions see Toolkit, page 120

AT THE TRAVEL CENTRE

All three celebrities in the programmes encounter difficulties (of different sorts!) when they make travel arrangements:

- Marcus gets confused at the bus station
- Ron is not really prepared at the car hire desk
- and Esther has not done her research before setting off.

What strategies could the three have used to overcome the obstacles they encountered? Some possibilities are:

- being assertive and sticking to your guns (Marcus)
- thinking ahead to what you might need to say and rehearsing it first (Ron)
- looking at some basic travel information on-line before walking all over town (Esther).

TRY IT OUT

Theme 4	*DVD*
Section 1:2	

Watch Esther arranging a journey at the train station, and pick out the specific ticket types she asks for. You can see the transcript and translation at the back of the book. As well as training your ear to spot details, listening is really useful in helping you to tune into the flow and sounds of the language too; French is not all about understanding every word and answering questions.

Be kind to yourself

Theme 4	*DVD*
Section 1:3	

So, you've rehearsed your question, and got it out word-perfect. Are you prepared for what you might hear in response? Often, you'll be able to predict the next logical step in the conversation. In this video clip, Marcus has a problem with his pronunciation. One of his words sounds like **horreurs** *(the horrors)* instead of **horaires** *(the timetable)* but his real problem comes when he is thrown by an unexpected question from the ticket person: **C'est pour quel trajet?** *(For which journey?)*. In the heat of the moment Marcus loses all his composure and forgets to think through the situation. If he was in an English bus station and asked for a ticket, what would he expect the other person to say? There are buses going all over the place, after all! She's simply asking where he is going. Marcus probably expected the word **voyage** for a journey, and was thrown by this synonym **trajet**. He couldn't work out that she was just asking the obvious next question!

– **Bonjour, mademoiselle.** *Good morning.*
  Monsieur. *Hello.*
– **Je voudrais un billet, s'il vous plaît.** *I'd like a ticket, please.*
  Oui, monsieur. C'est pour quel trajet? *Yes, (sir). Where are you going? (Which journey?)*
– **Euh ...** *(end of conversation)*

One strategy he could have tried was asking for clarification. He could have done this with some play-acting, raising the palms of his hands, shaking his head and saying one of the following:

Trajet? 'Trajet'?
Trajet? Je ne comprends pas 'trajet'. 'Trajet? I don't understand 'trajet'.
Trajet? Qu'est-ce que c'est? 'Trajet? What's that?

Or the old fallback:

Je suis anglais. Je ne comprends pas. S'il vous plaît, c'est quoi, 'trajet'?
I'm English. I don't understand. Please, what is 'trajet'?

The assistant may well then have searched for another way of conveying her message. You won't have a teacher with you to send you back to the desk like Marcus did, so you need to take the initiative and keep going.

If the assistant was speaking too quickly for him to get it all, he could have said:

Pouvez-vous parler plus lentement, s'il vous plaît? Could you speak more slowly please? or just **Plus lentement, s'il vous plaît.** More slowly please.

TRY IT OUT

Theme 4	_DVD_
Section 1:4	

By the end of the four weeks, Marcus masters the clarification technique. Watch him on stage in Marseilles when he is heckled by a **chasseur d'ours** (bear hunter). Can you spot what piece of French he uses to get himself out of that pressurised situation? It could be a very frequently-used expression for you as well! You can see the answer in the back of the book.

Theme 4	_DVD_
Section 2:14	

In the station, once you've worked out what the question means, you probably also need to:

* check the price: **C'est combien?** (How much is it?) or just **Combien?** (How much?)
* check what time the bus goes: **Le bus part à quelle heure?** (What time does the bus leave?) or just **À quelle heure?** (At what time?) might convey the message
* check which stop or bay it goes from: **Le bus part d'où?** (Where does the bus leave from?), or **Le bus part de quel arrêt?** (Which stop does the bus leave from?), or **Le bus part de quel quai?** (Which bay does the bus leave from?)
* check you're in the right place when you arrive: **Je cherche le bus pour Arles. C'est bien celui-là?/C'est bien ici?** (I'm looking for the bus to Arles. Is this it?/Am I in the right place?)

You can hear the phrases above on the DVD. At the train station, if you aren't using one of the ticket machines, you'll need to go to the **guichet** (ticket office), and maybe reserve a seat – **Je peux réserver une place?** – especially if you're travelling on a TGV (fast train).

TRY IT OUT

Theme 4
Section 2:15 *DVD*

Using the words below, and not forgetting your greetings etiquette, how would you:

1 ask for a first class no smoking single (ticket) to Nice?

2 ask for a second class return to Toulouse?

3 ask for a single (ticket) to Nice for today?

4 ask for a first class single (ticket) to Nice for tomorrow?

5 check the price?

You can see the answers at the back of the book, and hear them on the DVD.

un billet ticket

un aller simple single

un aller-retour return

classe class

première first

seconde/deuxième second

(non-)fumeur (no) smoking

pour for

aujourd'hui today

demain tomorrow

It takes a different sort of confidence to use the ticket machines that now abound in stations. Are you happier speaking to a real live person or dealing with a machine? That said, the text on screen may well provide clues you can read more swiftly than you can understand in speech. Still, be open-minded about the way information and choices are offered; it may not be word-for-word what you expect, and the language might be more formal and bookish than spoken French.

WORD ON THE STREET

(or in the station/airport/bus station)

These places are much the same the world over and many of the signs and notices you might guess, maybe with some lateral thinking:

Entrée

Toilettes

Contrôle des passeports

Point de rencontre (take the first *r-* off *rencontre*)

Départ immédiat

You can check your guesses at the back of the book. Some words you might need to know are not so guessable:

Accueil *Welcome desk*

Sortie *Way out*

Guichet *Ticket office*

Renseignements *Information*

Salle d'attente *Waiting room*

Déchets *Rubbish*

Consigne *Left luggage*

Location *Rental*

Défense de ... *Don't ...*

Obligatoire *Obligatory*

Compostez les billets *Stamp/validate your tickets*

One major difference between the system at stations in France and in the UK is that you are required to stamp your ticket at a **composteur** *(ticket punching machine)* before starting a journey – this is **obligatoire** and can lead to a fine if not done.

Make friends with your dictionary

We can be very literal-minded and expect there to be a word-for-word relationship between languages, yet in real life this is rarely the case. If you don't know a words, there may, however, be something you already know that you can recycle or adapt for the situation you find yourself in. This is especially the case if you can find an alternative way of saying what you mean. If you are able to identify a synonym, or other form of words to express it in English, you might well make the language leap to a parallel expression in French.)

When Marcus is in his taxi looking for the villa, he realises they've driven past it and wants to tell his *chauffeur* to go back. Instinctively he looks up 'back' in the dictionary. He finds the word that means a (person's) back, while what he really wants is 'go back'. Saying the equivalent of 'spine' in this situation would clearly not have been helpful.

If he'd thought laterally, he might have thought: Back? I don't know that. What else could I say in English? I mean 'go back' so I could say 'turn around' or, a bit more olde worlde, 'return'. Ah. Now I can try *retourner* or *retournez* in French. He did get as far as thinking 'turn around' and then 'turn' = *tourner*, or *tournez* in this situation (they both sound the same), but didn't know what to say when his driver wanted to know which way to turn.

The same sort of thing applies to other expressions in English:

'to write down', in French just *écrire*
'to listen out', in French just *écouter*
'to ring up', in French just *téléphoner*
'to carry on', in French just *continuer*

So, in the dictionary you need to read through the entry (don't stop at 'carry') until you find the word in the expression you want ('carry on').

This sort of process is the beginning of what Esther calls 'thinking in French', in other words, starting from what you do know how to say and then using it.

Theme 4	
Section 4	

DVD Challenge

Time for an interactive challenge. You are going to buy some tickets at the train station. Follow the prompts on screen to play your part in the conversation. You can see the transcript, as well as the translation, at the back of the book.

When trying to understand someone:

DO	DON'T
– look for clues in the context and in their face and gestures	– try to translate everything you hear
– try to extract and say back to them what you think are the key words	
– try to interpret (laterally) French words that sound like English	

When trying to make yourself understood:

DO	DON'T
– try to think of other ways of saying things	– stick at the first word you find in the dictionary
	– give up too easily

5

Going out

WHAT DO YOU WANT TO DO?

The kind of things you plan to do on your holiday will affect the type of language you need. In the programmes, some of the activities the celebrities need, or want, to do, include:

- socialising with each other and other people
- extending invitations
- joining in with local life
- going out to eat
- staying in to eat
- going to a cultural or sporting event.

It's worth taking time to think about places you may want to go, or things you may want to do on your trip abroad. You might want to:

- visit a stately house, castle, museum or ornamental garden
- watch a match or sporting event
- see an exhibition, a play, a classical concert, opera or ballet
- camp at an outdoor festival
- indulge your own personal interests.

All of these will mean you need to locate specialised language from the usual sources: your favourite website, dictionary, phrasebook or course material, depending on whether you're looking for the stalls or circle in the theatre, stands or boxes at a sporting fixture, or the mosh pit at a gig!

But don't forget, if your aim is to make your own language to suit your situation, and get what you want, it's also important to keep reminding yourself of things you do know how to say, and then adapt them to the new situation, rather than worry about things you don't know. There is a lot you can do in the context of sightseeing and going out, with French you've already seen in this book.

Be kind to yourself

Theme 5
Section 2:1
DVD

As usual, there is always French you know from other situations that you can use again when you're organising what you want to do. At the tourist office or visitor centre you could pick and mix to make up some sentences you need from this grid, never forgetting the essential opening gambit:

Bonjour (madame/mademoiselle/monsieur). C'est pour un renseignement ...

You can hear a selection of these sentences on the DVD.

Je voudrais ... *Je peux avoir ...* *Vous avez ...*	*un plan* *un dépliant* *un horaire* *une liste (des hôtels)*	*I'd like ...* *Can I have ...* *Have you got ...*	*a plan (map)* *a leaflet* *a timetable* *a list (of hotels)*
À quelle heure ...	*ouvre le château?* *ferme le château?*	*At what time ...*	*does the castle open?* *does the castle close?*
Qu'est-ce qu'il y a ...	*à voir ici?* *comme monuments?* *à faire pour les enfants?*	*What is there ...*	*to see here?* *in the way of sights?* *for the children to do?*
Est-ce qu'il y a ...	*des spécialités?* *une piscine?* *un endroit pour se baigner?* *un cinéma?* *un théâtre?*	*Is/Are there ...*	*any specialities?* *a pool?* *somewhere to go swimming?* *a cinema?* *a theatre?*

And not forgetting to end with *... **s'il vous plaît***.

TRY IT OUT

<table>
<tr><td>Theme 5</td><td rowspan="2">DVD</td></tr>
<tr><td>Section 2:2</td></tr>
</table>

To help you practise some specific questions that might come in handy, how could you ask:

1 for a list of restaurants?

2 if there is a campsite (**un camping**)?

3 for a leaflet in English?

4 if there is somewhere to walk (**se promener**)?

5 what time the park closes?

Suggested answers are at the back of the book, and you can hear them on the DVD.

WORD ON THE STREET

For some people, noticing the French around them in the street is a quick and natural way to acquire new words.

Musée d'Art Moderne
Horaires

lundi	de 10h00 à 12h30, de 14h30 à 18h00
mardi	fermeture hebdomadaire
mercredi	de 09h00 à 12h30, de 14h30 à 21h00
jeudi	de 10h00 à 12h30, de 14h30 à 21h00
vendredi	de 10h00 à 12h30, de 14h30 à 18h00
samedi	de 14h30 à 18h00
dimanche	de 14h30 à 18h00

From looking at the sign by the gate of this museum, you could probably work out the names of the days of the week in French. It might help to know that Sunday is the odd one out in the spelling pattern.

Opening times in some areas are a bit of a mystery, with local habits such as extended lunchtimes and festivals to take into account. Some specific expressions to look out for include:

ouvert open

tous les jours every day

un jour férié holiday (like a bank holiday)

une fête bank holiday, feast day (often religious)

fermeture hebdomadaire weekly closing day

> **OUVERT TOUS LES JOURS**
> **DE 10H00 À 12H00**
> **SAUF LUNDI ET FÊTES**

... and the very tricky **sauf** *(except)*, a word often in the small print but one which can suddenly change the whole text. Just when you thought it was safe to go in!

(Open every day, from 10am until midday, except Mondays and bank holidays/feast days)

As in English, in French people tell the time using both 24-hour and 12-hour clocks (although official train/flight departure times etc will always be given in the 24-hour version). In both versions in French, the hour part of the time is said first:

10am – **dix heures du matin** = 10h00 – **dix heures**

10pm – **dix heures du soir** = 22h00 – **vingt-deux heures**

Theme 5 / Section 2:3

When adding and taking away minutes (or quarter or half-hours) the French system works differently to the English. Instead of 'five past ten', the hour part of the time is said first. You can hear the following times on the DVD.

five past ten – **dix heures cinq** or
22h05 – **vingt-deux heures cinq**

ten past ten – **dix heures dix** or
22h10 – **vingt-deux heures dix**

quarter past ten – **dix heures et quart** or
22h15 – **vingt-deux heures quinze**

half past ten – **dix heures et demie** or
22h30 – **vingt-deux heures trente**

twenty to eleven – **onze heures moins vingt** or
22h40 – **vingt-deux heures quarante**

quarter to eleven – **onze heures moins le quart** or
22h45 – **vingt-deux heures quarante-cinq**

five to eleven – **onze heures moins cinq** or
22h55 – **vingt-deux heures cinquante-cinq**

As in English, there are special words for midnight (**minuit** = **zéro heures**) and noon (**midi** – also used to mean the South of France – **le Midi**).

Theme 5 / Section 3

TRY IT OUT

Now try an interactive activity on your DVD to practise understanding times. Listen out for the way people ask about times too. Transcripts and translations are at the back of the book.

The big differences

TALKING ABOUT THE FUTURE

In the programmes you'll hear many examples of people talking about things they are *going to do*, that is, about the future. As with English, French has a few ways of talking about the future, but perhaps the most simple and most useful in conversation is the one that corresponds exactly with the English:

je vais = I am going

regarder = to watch

<u>*Je vais regarder le football*</u> = <u>I am going</u> to watch the football.

Couldn't be simpler!

To make it into 'We're going to watch the football' use **on**, which you've seen before: **On va regarder le football**.

Or to ask someone, 'Are you going to watch the football?': **Vous allez/tu vas regarder le football?**

Use the Language Wheel below to practise some examples of what you're going to do. You can also hear them on the DVD.

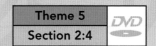

Theme 5	DVD
Section 2:4	

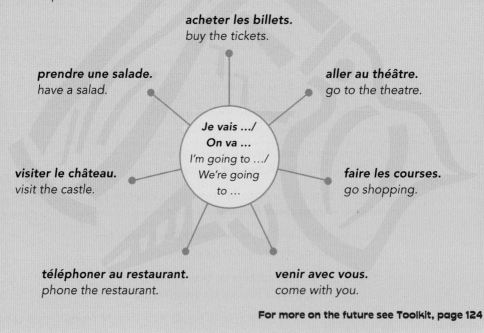

acheter les billets.
buy the tickets.

prendre une salade.
have a salad.

aller au théâtre.
go to the theatre.

**Je vais .../
On va ...**
I'm going to .../
We're going
to ...

visiter le château.
visit the castle.

faire les courses.
go shopping.

téléphoner au restaurant.
phone the restaurant.

venir avec vous.
come with you.

For more on the future see Toolkit, page 124

Some useful time expressions that you'll need when talking about the future are:

aujourd'hui today

demain tomorrow

ce soir tonight, this evening

cet après-midi *this afternoon*

ce week-end *this weekend*

Theme 5	DVD
Section 2:5	

TRY IT OUT

So, how might you say the following?

1 I'm going to visit a museum this afternoon.

2 We're going to go to a concert tomorrow.

3 We're going to see an exhibition this evening.

visiter *to visit*

aller *to go*

voir *to see*

une exposition *an exhibition*

You can see suggested answers at the back of the book, and hear them on your DVD.

Theme 5	DVD
Section 1:1	

Now watch this video clip, and see if you can pick out the expressions Florence uses to tell Esther what she is going to have to do.

As they are on good terms, she uses **tu**.

Transcripts and translations are at the back of the book.

INVITATIONS

If you want to invite someone to do something with you, you'll need the phrase: **Voulez-vous ...?** *(Would you like ...?)*.

You might want to use it in the classic phrase:
Voulez-vous sortir avec moi? *Would you like to go out with me?*

But you may not be up for this sort of invitation straight away. You might prefer to start your social challenges on safer ground.

There are, as you have seen before, two different forms of the word 'you' in French. This may be a context where it is much more appropriate to use the informal, friendly, affectionate form: **Tu veux ...?** *(Would you like ...?)* depending on who it is you are inviting.

In the Language Wheel on the next page are some ideas of things you might want to invite people to do. You can hear them on the DVD.

Theme 5	DVD
Section 2:6	

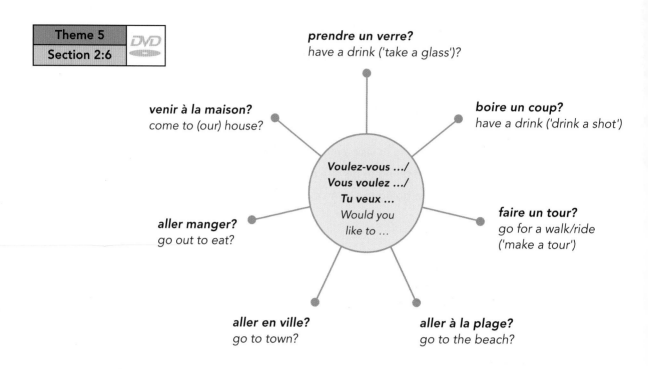

prendre un verre?
have a drink ('take a glass')?

venir à la maison?
come to (our) house?

boire un coup?
have a drink ('drink a shot')

Voulez-vous .../ Vous voulez .../ Tu veux ... *Would you like to ...*

aller manger?
go out to eat?

faire un tour?
go for a walk/ride ('make a tour')

aller en ville?
go to town?

aller à la plage?
go to the beach?

The big differences

IRREGULAR VERBS

Voulez-vous (or *vous voulez*) is an extremely useful part of the verb *vouloir* – 'to want', 'to wish'. As you saw before, when you look verbs up in grammar books or dictionaries, you find them in this form: *vouloir* – to want, but this is almost certainly not the part you need to use. You might want to say something like 'Do you want?' or 'I want' instead.

Most verbs in French follow a pattern, making it very easy to use them in the form you need – as you saw with *chercher* in Theme 2. However, some of the most common verbs are 'irregular' (*règle* = rule, so 'irregular' literally means 'not according to the rules'); and don't follow this pattern, so you have to learn them separately. English has irregular verbs too, of course (e.g. 'to be').

In the programmes we see Ron trying gallantly to memorise all six parts of the verb *aller* – but will he really need to use all of them? When you're focusing on speaking and understanding French, there aren't many verb forms you'll want to use regularly, and just two or three things you need to remember about the main ones (including how they sound). You've already seen a lot of them in the Language Wheels and dialogues in this book.

Of the six parts, the most useful to prioritise remembering are the *vous* part (to ask questions like 'Do you ...?', 'Have you ...?', 'Are you ...?', 'Are you going to ...?') and the *je* and *on* parts, to answer those questions. As your French improves and you start to develop friendships, you'll want to use the *tu* form as well.

For more on irregular verbs see Toolkit, page 122

Here is a top five of irregular verbs (you can see the verbs in full in the Toolkit):

From **pouvoir** (*to be able to*):
Vous pouvez …/Tu peux …? *Can you …?*
Je peux …/On peut … *I/We can …*

From **aller** (*to go*):
Vous allez …/Tu vas …? *Are you going (to) …?*
Je vais …/On va … *I'm/We're going (to) …*

From **avoir** (*to have*):
Vous avez …/Tu as …? *Have you (got) …?*
J'ai …/On a … *I/We have (got) …*

From **être** (*to be*):
Vous êtes …/Tu es …? *Are you …?*
Je suis …/On est … *I am …/We are …*

From **vouloir** (*to want*):
Vous voulez …/Tu veux …? *Do you want (to) …?*
Je veux …/On veut… *I/We want (to)*

Theme 5
Section 2:7

TRY IT OUT

Now, have a go at making some French sentences using these verbs. (For the 'you' questions, it's up to you whether you want to be polite **vous** or informal **tu**). Translate the phrases below to get you started.

1 Are you going to the match?

2 Are you going to the cinema?

3 Have you got any money?

4 Yes, I've got €20.

5 Are you on holiday?

6 Are you tired?

You can see suggested answers at the back of the book, and hear them on the DVD.

le match *the match*

l'argent *money*

fatigué(e) *tired*

en vacances *on holiday*

LES FÊTES

Festivals, parties, religious and other special events are all covered by the blanket term **une fête**. Dropping in on a local **fête** can give you a real insight into the community. In some parts of France they have **fêtes** celebrating local produce, such as **la fête du raisin** (grape festival), **la fête de la moule** (mussel festival), **la fête de la pêche** (peach festival), with tastings, music and traditional dress. If you're visiting France, check out the local tourist office website to see if your stay coincides with any special events – it could make it a memorable occasion.

Reading information on-line need not be too much of a nightmare, if you know what you are looking for, and keep your focus. You'll be looking crucially for:

- dates (you're probably not so interested if you're not going to be there)
- main features (could be a concert, parade, prize-giving).

TRY IT OUT

Here's some information about **fêtes** in Provence. Look first for the main sort of **fêtes**; what words do you spot? Then focus on the dates mentioned; what specific events are on? You can see the answers at the back of the book.

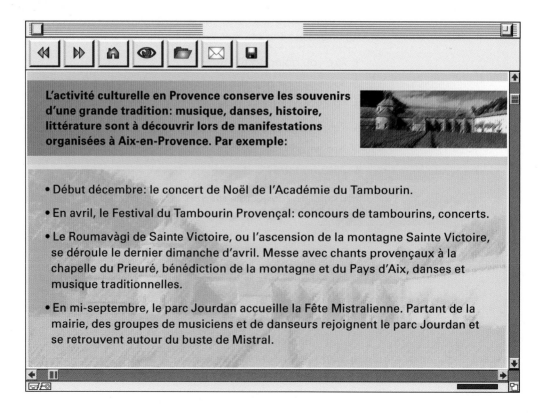

L'activité culturelle en Provence conserve les souvenirs d'une grande tradition: musique, danses, histoire, littérature sont à découvrir lors de manifestations organisées à Aix-en-Provence. Par exemple:

- Début décembre: le concert de Noël de l'Académie du Tambourin.

- En avril, le Festival du Tambourin Provençal: concours de tambourins, concerts.

- Le Roumavàgi de Sainte Victoire, ou l'ascension de la montagne Sainte Victoire, se déroule le dernier dimanche d'avril. Messe avec chants provençaux à la chapelle du Prieuré, bénédiction de la montagne et du Pays d'Aix, danses et musique traditionnelles.

- En mi-septembre, le parc Jourdan accueille la Fête Mistralienne. Partant de la mairie, des groupes de musiciens et de danseurs rejoignent le parc Jourdan et se retrouvent autour du buste de Mistral.

EATING OUT

| Theme 5 |
| Section 2:8 |

Getting ready for dinner can involve more than choosing what to wear and where to go! If you're in a restaurant in France you'll have to negotiate a variety of questions in the language as well.

Read the dialogue below, about deciding what to eat in a restaurant. You can also hear it on your DVD.

> – Bonsoir, monsieur.
> Messieurs-dames.
> – J'ai réservé une table pour trois personnes, au nom de Lewis.
> Bien sûr. Suivez-moi ... Voici la carte; les plats du jour sont affichés ici.
> – Excusez-moi. Je voudrais un conseil. On ne mange pas de viande; qu'est-ce que vous nous recommandez?
> Vous avez le choix: des pâtes, des salades, des quiches et des omelettes, si vous le désirez.
> – Et la bourride, qu'est-ce que c'est?
> C'est un plat de poisson typique.
> – Merci. On va prendre une salade à l'avocat, des tagliatelles... et pour moi ... euh ... je ne sais pas ... une quiche aux asperges.
> Et comme boisson?
> – Une carafe d'eau.
> De l'eau minérale?
> – Non, merci, de l'eau du robinet tout simplement.
> D'accord.

TRY IT OUT

Can you work out:

1 what general choices of food the diners have?

2 what advice they ask for?

3 what options the waiter offers?

4 why they ask about the **bourride**?

5 what they choose?

You can see the answers and a translation of the dialogue at the back of the book.

How would you personalise the French to give details of a reservation to suit you and your group? It's definitely worth rehearsing some of the customer lines with the DVD but, of course, in real life things rarely go this smoothly! You might choose a dish you don't like, be served food which is cold or overcooked; or it may start to pour down when you're seated on the terrace!

There are some things you can prepare for. You may be on a special diet, have specific food allergies you need to explain, or simply want to express your likes and dislikes. You can prepare for all this from your own reference sources or from the on-line resources on page 6. It may even be worth taking a written note in French to reassure you that, if you don't think you've made yourself understood in speech, you can flash the pre-written card to make everything clear.

As a general statement you could put on your card a note to say something like: **Je ne mange pas …** *(I don't eat …).*

You could then add an explanation, such as:

J'ai une allergie/Je suis allergique à … *I am allergic to …*
Je suis végétarien/végétarienne. *I'm vegetarian.*
Je fais un régime. *I'm on a diet.*
Je suis diabétique. *I'm diabetic.*

| Theme 5 | |
| Section 1:2 | |

The celebrities face their own challenges working in a restaurant, not least in keeping a smile on their faces. In her role as head waitress Esther gets a complaint about the temperature of the meal she has served, as you'll see in this video clip. First, listen out for the language she uses to check that she has understood the complaint from the customer and how she relates it to the chef. Then listen to the chef's response – Esther doesn't understand what he says, but picks up his tone very quickly. How does he feel and why? You can see answers and a transcript at the back of the book.

LET'S PRETEND

When you're away in France you can try the immersion technique yourself, making the effort to use a little bit more French every day and to do as many tasks as possible in French. At home it's harder, because it's not really natural to be speaking another language in such a familiar place. You could try role play though! You don't need to go the whole hog with costumes, but you could have a meal, or a party, or just a coffee with willing partners, and try to keep the conversation going **en français** *(in French).*

At this French gathering, you could challenge yourself to have a go at dealing with things that might happen in a restaurant, using some of the French you've met so far in this Theme. For example: ask for a menu, order from the menu or wine list, ask someone to pass the salt, complain or ask for help. The person playing the waiter could stir things up by bringing the wrong item, or something dirty or broken, in order to force people to use more French, or any other communication strategies (short of violence!).

Some of the main pieces of language a customer might need are:

S'il vous plaît ... (to attract attention or ask for something)
Il manque (un verre). There's (a glass) missing.
Je ne trouve pas (le sel). I can't find (the salt).
Je n'arrive pas à (ouvrir cette bouteille). I can't manage to (open this bottle).
Passez-moi (la carafe d'eau), s'il vous plaît. Pass me (the water jug) please.
Je peux avoir (une fourchette propre)? Can I have (a clean fork)?
Excusez-moi, ce verre est cassé/sale. Excuse me, this glass is broken/dirty.
Il me faut (une autre assiette). I need (another plate).

Theme 5	
Section 2:9	

You'll find some more useful restaurant words in the box below – you could label items on the table with these. You can hear how they're said on the DVD.

une assiette plate

un verre glass

un couteau knife

une fourchette fork

une cuillère à soupe soup spoon

une petite cuillère teaspoon

une carafe d'eau water jug

la carte menu

la carte des boissons drinks list

une serviette serviette

le pain bread (a staple on the French table)

de l'huile (some) oil

du vinaigre (some) vinegar

du sel (some) salt

du poivre (some) pepper

Theme 5	DVD
Section 1:3	

Even the celebrities have to get back to basics and learn the names of some essential restaurant crockery, as you'll see in this video clip of Esther undergoing waitress training.

TEACH AND TEST

Most of us forget something if we're only told it once, whether it's a person's name, a telephone number or some other information. It's exactly the same with French. In order to remember a word or phrase we need to repeat it, hear it, see it and use it many times in a short period in order to try to imprint it on our memory.

One way of doing this is to make and use some personalised 'Teach and Test' cards. All you need are some cards or pieces of paper, some language on a theme or in a situation you want to cover, and a pen or pencil. On one side of the card write the useful piece of French you want to memorise – it could be a word, a verb, a phrase or a sentence, or part of a Language Wheel. On the other side you draw a related picture to jog your memory, or write something in English that makes you think of the French you are practising.

Teach and test yourself; you could use all of these activities in this sequence, select the ones you like best, or invent your own:

- look at the French, and say it aloud or in your head
- look at the French and recall the English equivalent (and turn over to check)
- look at the English and turn over to check the French
- look at the English and recall the French equivalent (before you turn over to check)
- if it's language you might need to write, then try to write it down.

You could keep all of your cards in the same order if that helps you to memorise them, or add to the challenge by shuffling them. You can, of course, add other cards to your pack as you cover more language, and throw cards away as language sinks in. You can carry your cards around with you to have a look at while you're on the bus or standing in a queue, to make the most of your valuable time.

WHAT AM I LISTENING FOR?

A lot of the time, when you're trying to understand what someone is saying, you are just listening for the gist – the general sense. At other times you may be listening for a precise detail, e.g. a particular time or name, or the weather in your area. Gist can often be picked up not only from the spoken words themselves but also from what the speaker is doing – their facial expression, body language, something they are showing or pointing at, or other gestures. Think about the safety routine on planes, for instance. The point of the cabin crew going through the actions is to support the passengers' understanding of what the voiceover is about. The script itself is of secondary importance.

It's always worth checking detail by intervening during a rapid flow of French and repeating back key words to make sure that you've understood correctly. See the checking strategies in Theme 4.

Matching sound to writing is a skill you develop over time, and one that can help you identify things you already know when you hear them. Although French and English share many words that are written similarly, the sound systems are very different, and it may be that you don't recognise a familiar word because of the way it's pronounced. Getting used to the rules of pronunciation might help you to visualise what a spoken word looks like.

Of course you're not going to try to visualise every word you hear! That would be exhausting and pointless, and prevent you from joining in the conversation. Still, using this technique with words you hear often, or which seem to be particularly important, can help you recognise them. Use the pronunciation guide on the DVD to help you begin to get a visual picture of the sounds you hear in French. Now you've conquered the alphabet, you can always ask how an important detail word is spelled as well: **Comment ça s'écrit?** (remembering that not everyone is brilliant at spelling, even in their own language ...).

As you gain confidence you'll want to refine your listening skills by training yourself to listen out for key details. Imagine you're asking the waiter if they have your favourite dish:
Vous avez des moules? *Do you have mussels?*

The major thing you are listening out for is **oui** or **non**; if you don't hear either of those words you are going to need to check, ask him to repeat himself, or clarify what he said:
Vous avez des moules ... oui? *You have mussels ... yes?*

There are some frequently used words, though, that can radically alter the sense of what you hear, so as you get more used to hearing French you should be on the lookout (or 'listen-out') for these.

Consider the plight, for instance, of the person looking for the right bus to take him to the Palais des Papes in Avignon. He prepares his question, warms up with some potential replies, all for nothing if he fails to spot the crucial word that modifies the answer he gets:
Le bus pour Avignon part d'ici? *Does the bus for Avignon leave from here?*
Oui, monsieur ... mais il n'y a pas de bus aujourd'hui. *Yes ... but there are no buses today.*

If he only listens out for the key word (yes or no) he may not spot the vital **mais ...** *(but ...)* or the **pas** indicating a negative.

TRY IT OUT

| Theme 5 | DVD |
| Section 1:4 | |

For some listening practice, watch this clip of Esther besieging the locals with her British specialities.

1 First time round, try to pick up some French. Watch the whole scene and tune in to how she asks her question.

2 Next, listen for gist (the main message). What do the locals think of the specialities in general? Are they impressed? Remember you can listen to their tone of voice, look at their body language and facial gestures as well as listen to their words.

3 Next you can listen for detail. This is where you do need to pick out individual words. Esther is impressed by one particularly expressive word that she notes down. What do you think it means? Can you pronounce it? Using what you know about spelling in French, can you write it down?

You can see answers, as well as a transcript and translation, at the back of the book.

The big differences

NEGATIVE WORDS

Words that change the sense of a sentence radically are usually negative ones.

personne *nobody, no-one*

jamais *never*

rien *nothing*

plus *no longer, no more*

pas *not*

and, most sneakily, for the uninitiated:

que *only*

In proper written French these words are paired with the word **ne**, so you can spot them coming.

Je ne sais pas. *I don't know.*

Je ne comprends pas. *I don't understand.*

Le château n'ouvre que le matin. *The castle is only open in the mornings.*

You'll notice that the two parts of the negative are split up – usually by a verb.

In idiomatic spoken French the **ne** is often left out or not stressed enough to hear it. If it is there, it's often slurred.

J'sais (= Je ne sais) pas *I dunno (don't know)*

Beyond **ne ... pas**, which you have already met in Theme 3, the most useful negative words for you to be able to use are probably **rien**, **plus** and **jamais**. Have a look at the following sentences (you can also listen to them on the DVD) then have a go at using them yourself:

Theme 5	*DVD*
Section 2:10	

Vous ne savez rien. *You don't know anything.*

Je n'achète rien. *I am not buying anything.*

Il n'y a plus de chambres. *There are no more rooms.*

Je ne suis plus marié(e). *I am not married any longer.*

Tu n'as jamais d'argent. *You never have any money.*

Vous ne mangez jamais de viande? *Do you never eat meat?*

Theme 5	*DVD*
Section 2:11	

TRY IT OUT

How would you say these negative sentences?

1 I don't understand anything.

2 Don't you like anything?

3 I haven't got any more money.

4 I don't smoke any more.

5 I never work at the weekend.

l'argent *money*

fumer *to smoke*

travailler *to work*

le week-end *(at the) weekend*

You can see answers at the back of the book, and hear them on your DVD.

For more on negatives see Toolkit, page 125

Make friends with your dictionary

BUILD YOUR CONFIDENCE

As the connections between the English and French languages drifted apart over the centuries, following the huge imports of French into Britain after the Norman Conquest, so too spelling of shared words changed. But not so much that you won't be able to recognise some French words when you see them, especially if you use a bit of lateral thinking. So if you're looking at written French, in guidebooks or on-line, you might spot things that seem familiar. Using what you know of French, and the context, try guessing the word; this will make you less dependent on your dictionary.

Many words which in English start with 'dis-', in French start with **dé-**. Bearing this in mind, can you guess what the following words mean?

déconnecter	*désapprouver*
décourager	*désavantage*
découvrir	*désinfecter*

Of course, you might expect there to be a false friend among **dé-** words, and indeed there is. **Déception** nowadays means disappointment. (*'Deception'* is **tromperie** in French.)

English no longer uses accents in its alphabet (other than borrowed words like café or fiancé). Instead, many accents in the middle of words were replaced by the letter -s-.

TRY IT OUT

Armed with this insight, and a bit of context (and allowing some leeway for other changes over the centuries), you can probably work out what these words are in English:

intérêt (e.g. at a bank) and *dépôt*, too
vêtements (now used in French more generally than just for priests!)
fête (now used in French more widely than just eating)
hôpital (if the celebrations are too much)
conquête (in a campaign of war)
ancêtre (in your family tree)
forêt (for any other sort of tree)

More of a challenge:

dégoûtant (horrible)
détruit (after the campaign of war)
huîtres (on the seafood platter)

You can see translations of all these words at the back of the book.

Theme 5	
Section 4	

DVD Challenge

Time for an interactive challenge. Take part in this conversation with a friend about your plans for the weekend. Follow the prompts on screen to play your part. You can see the transcripts, as well as the translations, at the back of your book.

DO

– try to stay confident

– try different ways of learning and practising

– look around for new language – on signs, for instance

– guess at the meanings of words, using the rules and following the patterns that you know already, before you look them up in a dictionary

DON'T

– be surprised when things don't go to plan

– concentrate on what you *don't* know; think about what you *do* know

6
Getting on

SOCIALISING

One of the great pleasures of travelling is meeting other people, and getting involved in the local community. You might strike up a temporary holiday friendship with people you say **bonjour** to each day, or the French family in the same resort whose children get on with yours. In holiday mood people can be especially welcoming and sociable, and invite you to join in things you wouldn't normally try. There is a wealth of informal outdoor events that take place in sunny climes during the holiday and festival months, giving you plenty of opportunity to experience new things.

When you're in France, your main concern may well be to have a good time, relax, and soak up the culture, without having to worry about covering a syllabus, getting the details of your grammar spot on, or understanding every single word you hear. Nevertheless, having some basic social language to work with can increase your holidaying pleasure!

You may want to join in conversations and contribute to the **bonhomie** in the sort of way you would do at home. Indeed some people discover new aspects to their personality and become quite different social animals when they are abroad. You need to remember that you probably can't exchange the same banter and repartee that you could in your own language, but there are still things you could do that would make an impression and help you feel less like a spare part.

Some of the things you might like to do are:

- pay a compliment (about a place, food, someone's appearance)
- ask social questions and offer opinions
- talk about what you've been doing, tell a story or a joke
- join in a social activity (a game, a collective song, a special occasion, gossip)

- chat about common interests (food or travel, say)
- ask if you can help
- learn or teach a song
- recognise proper (and improper) French.

Making new language

BEING A GUEST

Theme 6
Section 2:1
DVD

If a French family invite you to join them for an **aperitif** (*l'apéro* for short) or visit their home, you'll want to make an effort, and ask what you can do to contribute to the **ambiance**. You're well-equipped to do this with a phrase you already know. Use **Je peux ...?** (*Can I ...?*) to offer a hand, or share out the workload by adapting it to **On peut ...?** (*Can we ...?*). Look at the Language Wheel for some examples of sentences you might want to say. You can also hear these on your DVD.

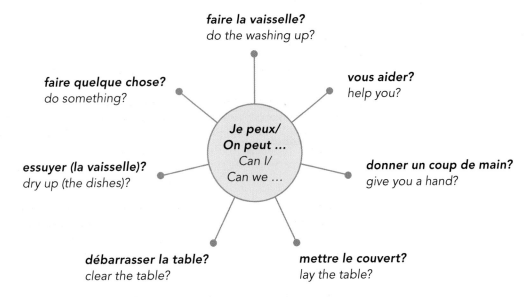

faire la vaisselle?
do the washing up?

faire quelque chose?
do something?

vous aider?
help you?

Je peux/ On peut ...
Can I/ Can we ...

essuyer (la vaisselle)?
dry up (the dishes)?

donner un coup de main?
give you a hand?

débarrasser la table?
clear the table?

mettre le couvert?
lay the table?

TRY IT OUT

Theme 6
Section 2:2
DVD

You could use **Je peux ...?** to make lots of useful sentences covering a variety of situations. Keep an open mind. You could be using this in a café, at a restaurant, in the hotel, at a bar, in conversation, out shopping or at the tourist office.

How might you ask if you can:

1 borrow a towel?
2 take this seat?
3 have a glass of water?
4 take a photo?
5 carry that for you?
6 have that one, please?

You can see suggested answers at the back of the book, and hear them on the DVD.

emprunter to borrow

apporter to carry

un verre glass

les mains hands

prendre to take, to have (food or drink)

avoir to have

une photo photo

une place seat

ce, cet, cette this

celui-là (m), celle-là (f) that one

une serviette towel

Theme 6
Section 2:3

As a polite guest, you'll no doubt want to compliment your hosts as well. **Vous avez ...**, without the question mark, is useful for this.

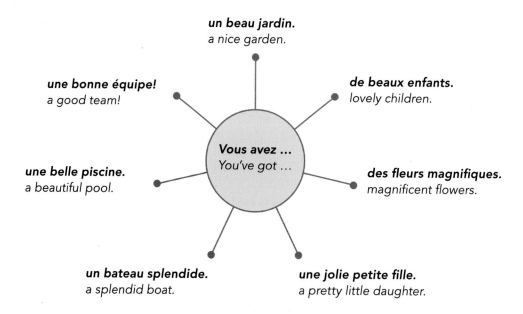

un beau jardin.
a nice garden.

de beaux enfants.
lovely children.

une bonne équipe!
a good team!

des fleurs magnifiques.
magnificent flowers.

Vous avez ...
You've got ...

une belle piscine.
a beautiful pool.

un bateau splendide.
a splendid boat.

une jolie petite fille.
a pretty little daughter.

Vous êtes ('you are', from the verb **être**, 'to be') is also useful when socialising.

Vous êtes très gentille. You're very kind.

Vous êtes très accueillant(e). You're very hospitable.

The big differences

ADJECTIVES

Have a look at the list of phrases in the table below. All the underlined words are adjectives – that is, words that describe something or someone – masculine on the left, feminine on the right. When you listen to them on the DVD you'll hear how the change in spelling also changes the sound. Knowing what you do about gender and agreement, look at the first four examples and see if you can work out the basic rule.

Theme 6	DVD
Section 2:4	

un mot <u>français</u>	la langue <u>française</u>
un musée <u>intéressant</u>	une exposition <u>intéressante</u>
un poivron <u>vert</u>	une pomme <u>verte</u>
le vin <u>rouge</u>	une pomme <u>rouge</u>
le vin <u>blanc</u>	une pêche <u>blanche</u>
un <u>vieux</u> château	une <u>vieille</u> maison
un <u>grand</u> pays	une <u>grande</u> ville
un <u>petit</u> peu	une <u>petite</u> maison
c'est un <u>beau</u> pays	c'est une <u>belle</u> ville
je suis très <u>heureux</u>	je suis très <u>heureuse</u>
il est <u>gentil</u>	elle est <u>gentille</u>

In your dictionary the adjective will be given with the masculine spelling: **vert**, **grand**, etc.

The basic rule is: if an adjective is describing something feminine you generally add an -**e** to the masculine spelling (unless it already ends in -**e**, as in **rouge**).

If it ends with the famous 'e acute', however, you still add an -**e** (as in **marié(e)**, 'married'), although you don't hear or pronounce it.

Some short common adjectives have their own rules (like **vieux/vieille**) – you'll find more in the Toolkit.

As in the examples given here, a lot of common adjectives (like colours) are placed after the thing they describe, as are longer words like **intéressant**. Others, like **grand** and **petit**, are placed in front. It's tough to remember, but usually clicks into place when you hear it, and not life-threatening if you say it the other way around.

For more on adjectives see Toolkit, page 119

Theme 6	DVD
Section 2:5	

CHEERS!

The *apéritif* is a very important social event, and an ideal opportunity for interaction with other people. It can be a drink, or a drink with snacks, before any meal, and it can be very protracted, especially in the warmer months when people eat later in the evening.

As for toasts, you'll find these useful:

Joyeux anniversaire! Happy Birthday!
Félicitations! Congratulations!
Bonne fête! Have a good party! (Also used to mean 'Happy saint's day!')
À votre santé! Your health!
À la vôtre! Cheers! (literally, 'To yours!')
Bonne santé, tout le monde! To everyone's good health!

Theme 6	DVD
Section 1:1	

Esther finds much inspiration in her *apéritif*. Watch this clip of her interviewing Michel Bosque, a pastis expert, and see if you can pick out how she toasts him and how she describes the taste of the drink. You can see the answers, a transcript and a translation at the end of the book.

Because the *apéritif* is so well-established, there are even devices to get people to have another drink. Once you've had your first drink it is not uncommon for the host to cajole you by saying something like: ***Vous n'allez pas marcher sur une jambe*** (You're not going to walk on one leg), implying you have to balance things by having a second drink.

USING WHAT YOU'VE GOT

One of the great skills of communicating in this sort of environment (or indeed any environment) is being able to maintain the flow of conversation. It's important to reassure the person you're talking to that they have your undivided attention. Your body language and listening skills can help you out here!

You don't have to do all of the talking; once you've run out of pre-prepared things to chat about you can still carry on the conversation for a decent time just using active listening skills. For example, you can nod, sigh or tut in the right places, express agreement **Oui, oui** (Yes, yes) or surprise **Non! Vraiment?!** (No! Really?!) from time to time, or make those 'I am listening' noises: 'ah...', 'oh ...', 'mmm ...'. The words below will do the trick. You can also hear them on your DVD.

Theme 6	DVD
Section 2:6	

Alors ... So ...
Et alors? So, what's the meaning of that?
Ben ... (or *eh bien*) Well then ...
C'est-à-dire ... Well, I mean ...
C'est ça. That's right.
Comment? Pardon?
D'accord. OK.

Use them to mark hesitation and keep the conversation flowing. Learn one or two and drop them into your conversation to sound more French. Don't worry if you don't say as much as everyone else. Some people like to have an audience and, if you can manage to listen to them for a good period and stay looking interested, they'll be convinced you're a fluent French speaker!

When you get more confident you can begin to reflect back the language you hear around you, repeating certain key words. This makes it appear as if you are contributing more than you really are. You can even begin to guess what someone might say to complete a sentence. Marcus is a good example of someone who actively listens, and tries to recycle words he picks up straight away; Ron is a good model of someone who takes the route of communicating through other channels.

Pause for thought

If you do get stuck for a word that just lingers on the tip of your tongue, you could try a couple of strategies. A word well-used in French is **le machin** *(the thingy)* which can fill a gap in any sentence. **Passez-moi le ...** (can't think of the word for 'corkscrew') **... le machin** (with fevered unscrewing mime!) *(Pass me the ... thingy.)*

If you can't think of one word but do remember another that's related (what the thing's used for, for instance) you can paraphrase. **Passez moi le ...** (still can't remember the word for 'corkscrew') **... pour ouvrir la bouteille.** *(Pass me the ... for opening bottles.)*

Or something that's not a mile off but you know isn't right: **Passez moi le ...** (What *is* the word for corkscrew?) **... pas l'ouvre-boîtes mais le ... pour ouvrir la bouteille.** *(Pass me the ... not the tin-opener but the ... for opening bottles.)*

THE CHAT

Theme 6
Section 1:2

In informal social situations there's a lot of general chitchat (French has an expressive verb for this – **tchatcher**). As usual, if you want to be involved from time to time in the social mix, you can recycle the French you know and prepare some exchanges to fall back on, as Esther does during her TV interview with politician Jack Lang. She always has an escape route (not silence) so that he doesn't get the chance to start talking at great length and great speed.

What Esther does is:

- prepare a basket of gifts, and something to say about each of them
- link them to questions she already knows
- keep control of the interview by going at her own pace and not proceeding until she is ready.

Watch Esther's final challenge and pick out what she says to structure the interview so that she stays in charge. What comments does she begin with, and what questions does she follow up with? Finally, play the clip again, and see if you can speak at the same time as Esther, using her words. You can try this with the sound on as a guide, or with it turned off for more of a challenge. You can see the answers, along with translations of the key language, at the back of the book.

To prepare for a social conversation of your own, you may want to:

- remind yourself of everyday greetings and routines, e.g. asking how people are
- prepare language which will give some background on your own family, home, work or previous travelling
- prepare some observations on what you've experienced during your time in France and comparisons with back home
- think of some follow-up questions to statements on topics you can cope with or are interested in (or ideally, both!) so that you can take the initiative and prolong an exchange.

Theme 6	DVD
Section 2:7	

You can see some examples below of how to expand on an initial conversation opener, and hear them on your DVD.

Statement	Follow-up question
Bonjour. Je m'appelle Joan. *Hello. I'm Joan.*	**Et vous?** *And you are?*
On est allé à Toulon aujourd'hui. *We went to Toulon today.*	**Vous connaissez Toulon?** *Do you know Toulon?*
J'ai bien aimé l'exposition sur la place. *I enjoyed the exhibition in the square.*	**Qu'est-ce que vous en pensez?** *What do you think of it?*

The big differences

ASKING QUESTIONS

When Ron met a taciturn barman, he needed a strategy to get him to talk. Being able to ask some questions would have helped. Some of the key question words in French are:

Pourquoi ...? Comment ...? Quand ...?
Qui ...? Où ...? Qu'est-ce que ...? Quel(le) ...?
Why ...? How ...? When ...? Who ...? Where ...?
What ...? Which ...?

As usual there are different ways of asking the same question, including finding a word order that sounds good to you:

Où habitez-vous?
Vous habitez où?
Où est-ce que vous habitez?

all mean exactly the same thing (*Where do you live?*) and are equally correct!

Likewise, to find out what time the train leaves, you can ask:

À quelle heure part le train?
Le train part à quelle heure?

Look at these ways of asking about what people have been doing, listen to them on the DVD and then have a go yourself.

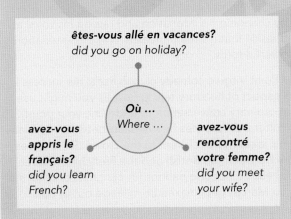

êtes-vous allé en vacances?
did you go on holiday?

Où ...
Where ...

avez-vous appris le français?
did you learn French?

avez-vous rencontré votre femme?
did you meet your wife?

Theme 6	DVD
Section 2:8	

vous avez vu à Marseille?
did you see in Marseille?

Qu'est-ce que ...
What ...

vous avez fait en vacances?
did you do on holiday?

vous avez choisi?
have you chosen?

êtes-vous allé en Chine?
did you go to China?

Pourquoi ...
Why ...

avez-vous aimé le film?
did you like the film?

avez-vous invité le chef?
did you invite the chef?

TRY IT OUT

Now try these conversational gambits:

1 Where did you have dinner yesterday evening?

2 What did you eat at the restaurant?

3 Why did you choose that restaurant?

You can see the answers at the back of the book, and hear them on the DVD.

For more on asking questions see Toolkit, page 126

Theme 6	DVD
Section 2:9	

TRY IT OUT

Theme 6	DVD
Section 1:3	

When Esther has the challenge of interviewing the people of Cavaillon about their opinions of British people moving into the area, she doesn't get it quite right. Watch this video clip to see what question she asks.

How could you adapt the question to ask:

1 What do you think of the football match?

2 What do you think of the concert?

3 What do you think of the wine?

4 What do you think of the restaurant?

Theme 6	DVD
Section 2:10	

You can see suggested answers at the back of the book, and hear them on the DVD.

le match de football football match

le concert concert

le vin wine

Be kind to yourself

Telling a joke in another language, as Marcus discovers, is one of the hardest challenges you can set yourself. Simply translating one you already know doesn't work, as jokes often rely on word play, and puns don't exist in the same way in French. When Marcus finally does crack it and get a laugh, it's because he's adapted his performance to fit in with his linguistic abilities. The same goes for you; try to use language you know and adapt it to your situation. When Marcus first approaches strangers with his blonde joke, he struggles as long as he relies on the words alone to do the job. He manages to get a laugh in the end by changing his intonation and raising his voice at the end of the joke to emphasise that it's the punchline! Timing, intonation and body language are powerful tools.

In his final challenge in the Point Virgule comedy club in Paris, his success is largely due to the physical aspect of his story telling (just as you might use gestures or signs in a more ordinary conversation to underline your point). He also bases his humour on cultural differences he's noticed between Parisians and Provençaux, to make his jokes more relevant to the crowd. Differences, competitiveness and rivalry between the British and the French have been the sources of humour for these competing nations for centuries and are still a good source of teasing, so Marcus gets maximum mileage out of the Olympics rivalry.

Our resident football expert Ron is very limited in the amount of (French) language he can use accurately and appropriately; yet still he manages to be entertaining company, and to remain part of the **équipe** *(team)*.

Theme 6
Section 2:11

Footballing jokes around the world tend to be quite cruel, like this one, told at the expense of Paris Saint-Germain (PSG), the team Ron sees playing at Parc des Princes in his final challenge. Try to read the French version, with the help of the vocabulary, before you look at the translation at the back of the book. Remember to think about words that look a bit like English. You can also hear it on your DVD.

> On regarde le match dans un bar sur le grand écran - PSG contre l'OM. Tout près, devant l'écran, un type est assis avec son chien; le type boit un pastis; le chien a les yeux fixés sur le match. Quand PSG prend le ballon et fait une avance, le chien se lève et se met à aboyer; plus PSG s'approche du but, plus il aboie. Quand le joueur parisien perd le ballon, le chien s'assied et se calme.
>
> Le barman dit au type: "Il est formidable, votre chien! Qu'est-ce qu'il fait quand ils marquent un but?".
>
> Le type répond: "Ah ça, je ne sais pas; ça ne fait que six mois que je l'ai."

It could equally be told of any other team having a bad, goal-less season.

le grand écran *big screen*

le type *guy, bloke*

les yeux *eyes*

une avance *advance*

aboyer *to bark;* **il aboie** *he barks*

le but *goal*

plus *more*

perd *loses*

qu'est-ce qu'il fait? *what does he do?*

marquer un but *to score a goal*

The big differences

TALKING ABOUT THE PAST

When Marcus comes back from his fruitless walk around the castle in Fontaine-de-Vaucluse (built, he claims, by monkeys in the Middle Ages!) he bemoans to his teacher that he hasn't had a chance to practise his *passé composé* – not a complaint you hear every day!

The *passé composé* (also called the perfect tense) is the form you give to a verb to talk about the past, as Marcus was doing at the castle, or as you might do when you are talking about how you've spent the day, or when telling stories, anecdotes or jokes.

Some examples starting with *Je* (I):

J'ai travaillé I worked, I have worked

J'ai fini I finished, I have finished

J'ai vu I saw, I have seen

J'ai dormi I slept, I have slept

You'll see that in English there is more than one form, while in French there is only the one, and it always has an extra word in the middle. This extra word is referred to in reference works as an auxiliary verb (from Latin 'auxiliare' to help – it helps to show it's the past tense).

The auxiliary verb is not always *J'ai* (which is part of *avoir* – 'to have') but it's certainly very common, as you'll soon see.

French past participles tend to end either in *-é* or in *-i* or in *-u* (as here), but, as always, there are some exceptions.

For more on the passé composé see Toolkit, page 123

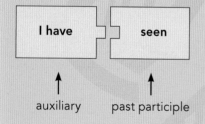

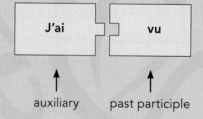

You use this *passé composé* tense in conversation to talk about what you have been doing in the day or things you did in the past. You can also use it to make questions (using *vous avez*) to find out what people have been doing, what sights they've seen or things they've heard. You can see some examples in the Language Wheel below, and hear them on your DVD.

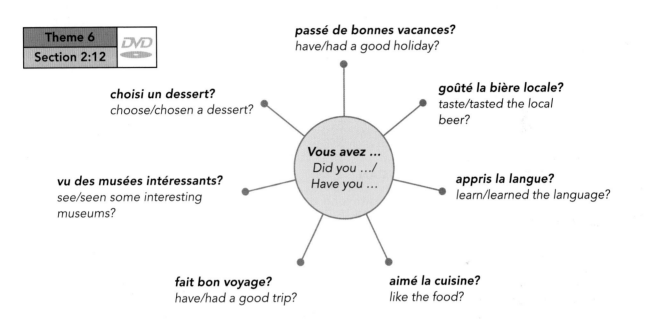

Theme 6	DVD
Section 2:12	

passé de bonnes vacances?
have/had a good holiday?

choisi un dessert?
choose/chosen a dessert?

goûté la bière locale?
taste/tasted the local beer?

vu des musées intéressants?
see/seen some interesting museums?

Vous avez ...
Did you .../
Have you ...

appris la langue?
learn/learned the language?

fait bon voyage?
have/had a good trip?

aimé la cuisine?
like the food?

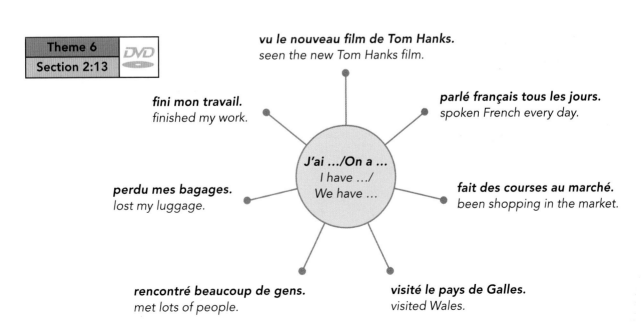

Theme 6	DVD
Section 2:13	

vu le nouveau film de Tom Hanks.
seen the new Tom Hanks film.

fini mon travail.
finished my work.

parlé français tous les jours.
spoken French every day.

J'ai .../On a ...
I have .../
We have ...

perdu mes bagages.
lost my luggage.

fait des courses au marché.
been shopping in the market.

rencontré beaucoup de gens.
met lots of people.

visité le pays de Galles.
visited Wales.

The big differences

MORE TALKING ABOUT THE PAST

Now for the tricky matter of verbs that don't use part of **avoir** as their auxiliary. There aren't many of these, but they are quite common, as they nearly all deal with movement. Possibly the most useful is:

Je suis allé(e) *I went, I have been*

With these verbs (the others are listed in the Toolkit) the auxiliary is part of **être**, the verb *'to be'*. The trap for English speakers is that, if you are translating word for word, you might think **Je suis** always means *'I am'*, and so mistranslate **Je suis allé(e)** as *'I am going'*. When **Je suis** is with another verb, as it is here, it doesn't mean *'I am'*, but shows a sentence in the past tense.

For the most common verbs in their passé composé form see Toolkit, page 123

YOU CAN-CAN

Theme 6	DVD
Section 2:14	

For those who like tongue twisters and are real gluttons for punishment, here's a musical challenge. This version of the can-can outlines the rules for the **passé composé** and brings together examples of some of the common verbs too. Your challenge is to join in and keep up!

> Le passé composé
> il est constitué
> d'un participe passé
> avec un auxiliaire.
>
> Ce participe passé
> finit souvent en -é.
> (Mais quelquefois en -i et -u aussi.)
>
> J'ai choisi, j'ai mis, j'ai pris,
> j'ai dit, j'ai ri, je suis sorti.
> J'ai fini, j'ai compris,
> j'ai mis, j'ai pris,
> j'ai dit, j'ai ri.
>
> J'ai voulu, j'ai pu,
> j'ai vu, j'ai dû, j'ai bu, je suis venu.
>
> J'ai reçu, j'ai perdu,
> j'ai pu, j'ai vu, j'ai dû, j'ai bu.

Le passé composé
il est constitué
d'un participe passé
avec un auxiliaire.

Ce participe passé
finit souvent en -é.
(Mais quelquefois en -i et -u aussi.)

The passé composé
is made up of
a past participle
with an auxiliary.

This past participle
often ends in -é.
(But sometimes in -i and -u as well.)

I chose, I put, I took, (I've chosen, I've put, I've taken),
I said/told, I laughed, I went out (I've said/told,
I've laughed, I've been out).
I finished, I understood, (I've finished, I've understood),
I put, I took, (I've put, I've taken),
I said/told, I laughed (I've said/told, I've laughed).

I wanted, I was able, (I've wanted, I've been able),
I saw, I had to, I drank, I came, (I have seen, I've had to,
I've drunk, I've come).

I received, I lost, (I've received, I've lost),
I was able, I saw, I had to, I drank, (I've been able, I've seen,
I've had to, I've drunk).

The passé composé
is made up of
a past participle
with an auxiliary.

This past participle
Often ends in -é.
(But sometimes in –i and – u as well.)

To start with you could just try to read the verses aloud, then play the DVD and try to keep up! If you get good at it, you can start to work from the English words on this page, trying to say the equivalent in French at the pace of the music. **Bonne chance!** (Good luck!).

JOINING IN: SINGING ALONG

Theme 6	DVD
Section 1:4	

The words of the French national anthem, the Marseillaise, which Marcus tries to learn in this clip, are famously bloody and violent, as indeed most national anthems are jingoistic and nationalistic. If you do hear it sung, it's likely to be only the first verse, as many people don't remember the words beyond that. It's easy to get carried away in a crowd and start to sing along, although it may feel weird to be singing about the impure blood of the enemy, when that enemy historically might have been you! It would be equally strange for French people to sing the British national anthem, asking God to save a monarch they got rid of three centuries ago. However, those martial rhythms can be quite compelling!

The words you might like to join in with are underlined:

<u>Allons enfants de la patrie;</u>
<u>le jour de gloire est arrivé.</u>
Contre nous de la tyrannie
l'étendard sanglant est levé,
l'étendard sanglant est levé.
Entendez-vous, dans les campagnes,
mugir ces féroces soldats?
Ils viennent jusque dans vos bras
égorger vos fils, vos compagnes.

<u>Aux armes citoyens!</u>
<u>Formez vos bataillons!</u>
<u>Marchons, marchons.</u>
Qu'un sang impur
abreuve nos sillons.

Arise children of the fatherland;
the day of glory has arrived.
Against us the bloody standard of tyranny is raised. (repeated)
Can you hear the sound in the fields,
the howling of these ferocious soldiers?
They are coming into our homes (arms)
to cut the throats of your sons and consorts.

To arms, citizens!
Form your batallions!
Let's march, let's march.
Let impure blood
flow in our fields. (irrigate our furrows)

You could try declaiming this as pronunciation practice. Poetry and songs can be a good vehicle for improving your sense of the rhythm and flow of French, because of their structure. Check out www.marseillaise.org to hear the anthem sung in full.

There may be other, less politically charged songs you'll come across, depending on the situations you find yourself in. 'Happy Birthday' is pretty universal, and the French do sometimes sing it in English. There are also at least two French versions, sung to the same tune. The easiest one goes:

Joyeux anniversaire,
Joyeux anniversaire,
Joyeux anniversaire, (name)
Joyeux anniversaire!

At a birthday party the song usually comes with the dessert or sometimes with the **apéritif**. Drinking songs are especially popular at big social occasions like weddings, parties, post-match drinks or seasonal **fêtes** *(festivals)*, like **la fête du village** *(village festival)* or **la fête du vin** *(wine festival)*. The main requirement for participants here is not to have a wide range of vocabulary and perfect grammar, but to be able to partake copiously of the drinks available and to laugh at appropriate times! In the final programme we see a great example of the football team toasting Ron in song, proving that you don't need to know a lot of French to be popular.

PARTY PIECE

Theme 6	DVD
Section 2:15	

A party piece could be a good way to immerse yourself in French company, as well as give you valuable pronunciation practice! It could be a verse from a song, a joke or story or something else, like a tongue-twister. You could try to learn and perform one in French. Here are some examples. You can also hear them on your DVD.

> petite truite cuite, petite truite crue
>
> des antiquités authentiques
>
> un bon chasseur, sachant chasser,
> doit savoir chasser sans son chien
>
> little cooked trout, little raw trout
>
> authentic antiques
>
> a good hunter, who knows how to hunt,
> must know how to hunt without his dog

Like English tongue-twisters, they don't make much sense, and they are not tongue-twisters in English when translated word for word.

You could try to teach French people a tongue-twister in English, like 'Peter Piper' or 'She sells seashells'. The trickiest sounds for French people to reproduce are those they don't use themselves, of course, such as the '-ie' as in pie, '-th' as in mouth, or 'th-' as in then.

Another source of interest might be long words; English has a larger vocabulary than French and because of its mixed history has some really long words you can impress your hosts with: floccinaucinihilipilification (honest – you can look it up). In French, one they are quite likely to challenge you with is: **anticonstitutionnellement** (anti-constitutionally), supposedly one of the longest words in their dictionary.

I'VE GOT YOUR NUMBER

So, you have managed your **apéritif** conversation wonderfully, you've articulated and pronounced clearly, you've joined in the singing, offered to help, wowed people with your party piece and hit it off with someone. What if they now want to get in touch?

If someone gives you a telephone number in French they usually group the figures together to make them easier to remember. So, instead of separating them out as we would in English:

0-2-0-8-7-5-2-5-5-2

they would say
02 - 08 – 75 – 25 – 52.

(zéro deux, zéro huit, soixante-quinze, vingt-cinq, cinquante-deux)
(zero two, zero eight, seventy-five, twenty-five, fifty-two)

You'd be expected to do the same thing with your phone number. The same pattern applies to other long strings of numbers, such as codes for collecting pre-booked tickets.

TRY IT OUT

Theme 6	
Section 2:16	

How would you say these numbers? You can hear them on your DVD, and see them written as words in the back of your book.

04 – 74 – 27 – 46 – 99
03 – 04 – 55 – 23 – 78
02 – 64 – 33 – 66 – 12

How would you give your own phone number?

If someone is giving you a number in French, use all your slowing down, checking and repeating strategies to get as many chances as possible of picking it up right. On the phone, the standard greeting is **Allô** (Hello). To say who you are, simply say **Ici ...** (Here ...) plus your name. **Je m'appelle** (My name is) is used in more formal situations. You might also ask:

Qui est à l'appareil? Who is calling (on the machine)?
C'est de la part de qui? Who is calling? (Who is it on behalf of?)

Theme 6	DVD
Section 3	

TRY IT OUT

Time for an interactive challenge. On your DVD you'll hear three different answering machine messages. You need to listen out for the phone numbers you are asked to contact. You can see transcripts and translations at the back of the book.

TALKING BASIC (VERY BASIC) FRENCH

As we know from Ron and Marcus' examples, in the heat of the moment and under pressure, it's easy to pick the wrong word or to hear something unexpected coming out of your mouth! If you spot it you can, of course, correct it or indeed make light of it by saying it again in a tone, and with a dramatic flourish, that expresses the sense: 'Where did that come from?'

This sort of thing can happen particularly with words or phrases that sound a bit like each other, as in the case of the British visitor who, having observed a French boules game at the village **piste** (not as bad as it sounds – it's just the ground or rink), joined in and actually won a game of **pétanque.** In his excitement he announced to the assembled locals: **Je suis le champignon!** (*I am the mushroom!*) The word he searched for was obviously **champion**; equally obviously the people around could see the funny side and understand what he really meant.

Marcus' slip of the tongue in the restaurant when he asks for four **connards** instead of four **canards** (*ducks*) illustrates the importance of having clear vowels. The word he used is heard regularly in road rage situations, and implies stupidity, allied with obstinacy and an inability to keep your mouth shut, not a combination of social skills to aspire to!

The French are keen on insults to do with lack of intelligence, eccentric behaviour, illness or madness, and are not at all PC about it. You might hear (hopefully not directed at you) words like:

cinglé crazy
malade sick
fou mad
imbécile idiot

all of which have these connotations.

You may need to recognise some of these (the list goes on ...) to be able to escape confrontational situations. It's recommended that you don't use them yourself!

Make friends with your dictionary

Dictionaries can be dangerous! For one thing when you look in an English-French dictionary, you have to pick the right half! For another, when you find the word you want, there are sometimes several different words under the same heading. Which one do you pick? Moreover, in French you may have to look for extra clues before you can use the word.

If it's a noun is it **le** or **la** or **les**?
If it's a verb what do I need to add to the form written in the book?
If I say it as it is, will anyone understand?

A good way to check if you have the word you want (if you're using a French-English, English-French dictionary) is to cross-reference: look up the French words you've found in the other half of the book; the explanations in English often give you a sense of how that word is used.

For example, say you want to tell someone that the place you have visited on the coast is 'a nice spot'. First, you could think around the phrase, to see if any French words you know would do instead. You might decide 'beautiful' or 'good' would do instead of 'nice'. You might also decide that 'place', 'town', 'beach' (or whatever the spot is) could replace 'spot', and you'd be right – 'spot' is one of those difficult-to-deal-with English idioms that might be better replaced with a more precise word.

However, say you decide to look up 'spot' in your English-French dictionary anyway. You could find dozens of words, including:

Spot – **tache (f)**

– **éclaboussure (f)**	– **goutte (f)**
– **pois (m)**	– **bouton (m)**
– **point (m)**	– **un peu de ...**
– **souillure (f)**	– **endroit (m)**
– **salissure (f)**	

depending on the exact usage (a spot in a pattern, a spot of dirt, a spot of rain, a spot of light exercise, a measles spot etc.) If your dictionary is good it might explain the differences; if not, you should cross-reference to the French part to check other English translations of each word to eliminate the unhelpful suspects. If you were to say **une belle tache**, for example, this means 'a big dirty mark', hardly the ringing endorsement you were aiming for!

In this case, **un bel endroit** (a nice place) would be the best option for the sense of 'spot' that you want.

Theme 6	
Section 4	

DVD Challenge

Time for an interactive challenge on your DVD. You're chatting to a French friend about his trip to Britain. Follow the prompts on screen to play your part. You can see the transcript, as well as the translation, at the back of the book.

DO

- leave your bushels of notes behind; just take your basics

- think about things apart from language that help you communicate

- share the experiences and emotions on the films, and share the ups and downs of your own challenges – you're not alone!

- try out some of the learning strategies you've read about in this book; you can't judge if they suit you without giving them a go

DON'T

- give up – stick to your guns, check and clarify

- expect to be spoon-fed – people will talk fast

- try to translate everything from English – think of simple things you might be able to say

- give in; if people talk to you in English keep trying to use your French when you can

And finally, some advice the celebrities might have given:

RON
Don't discount the Harpo Marx technique – it served me well!
Pas de problème *(No problem).*

ESTHER
Don't be too British; when you're ready, swallow your reserve and take the conversational stage.

MARCUS
Don't take your mistakes too seriously. ***C'est pas mal pour un Anglais*** *(It's not bad for an Englishman).*

Toolkit

This Toolkit picks up on 'The big differences' sections from the Themes and expands on them where appropriate. It also contains a pronunciation guide.

Gender

In French, all nouns, whether they are objects or people, have a gender – they are either masculine or feminine.

Gender is seen (and heard) in particular words:

• in articles (words like 'the' and 'a') – so *'a man'* is <u>**un** homme</u> and *'a woman'* is <u>**une** femme</u>.
• in adjectives, words that describe the nouns (see Adjectives).

Words like 'my' and 'your' (possessives) are also among the words that show the gender link. So *'my car'* is always <u>**ma** voiture</u> whether you are a man or a woman ... because **voiture** *(car)* is always feminine.

	+ masculine word	+ feminine word	+ any singular word starting with a vowel or silent 'h'	+ any plural word
the	le	la	l'	les
my	mon	ma	mon	mes
your (friendly form)	ton	ta	ton	tes
your (polite form)	votre	votre	votre	vos
our	notre	notre	notre	nos
to the	au	à la	à l'	aux
of the/some	du	de la	de l'	des

The words meaning 'this' or 'that' have a slightly different pattern:

	+ masculine word	+ feminine word	+ a masculine singular word starting with a vowel or silent 'h'	+ any plural word
this/that	ce	cette	cet	ces

Ce livre can mean *'this book'* or *'that book'*. To make it more precise, you might hear or use: *ce livre-ci* (*this book here*) as opposed to *ce livre-là* (*that one over there*).

In *cette assiette* (*this plate*) and *cet homme* (*this man*) the first word sounds the same; when it's written down you can see the difference between a feminine spelling (for *assiette*) and the spelling before a masculine word starting with a vowel or silent 'h' (*homme*).

Singular and plural

Singular refers to one thing, person, place etc. and plural to more than one. In English you can see and hear the difference, even if not all words follow the same pattern:

a melon – melons
the carrot – the carrots
a woman – women
the mouse – the mice

In French, you see the difference rather than hear it (as the final **-s** is silent). Instead, the plural is heard in the word that comes before: **des** (some); **les** (the); **mes** (my) etc.

un melon – **des** melons *a melon – some melons*
une carotte – **des** carottes *a carrot – some carrots*

le melon – **les** melons *the melon – the melons*
la carotte – **les** carottes *the carrot – the carrots*

Although most words in French add an **-s** in the plural, there are some unusual forms including words ending in **-al**: **un animal** (an animal) becomes **des animaux** (animals).

Words ending in **-eau** (**le cadeau**, present) or **-eu** (**le jeu**, game) add an **-x** (**les cadeaux**, presents, **les jeux**, games), but again you can't hear the difference as the final **-x** is also silent.

Adjectives

Adjectives describe nouns (big, red, old etc). Adjectives have both a feminine and masculine form and you choose the form that matches – or agrees with – the gender of the noun; if the noun is masculine, the adjective is in the masculine form and if the noun is feminine, the adjective will also be in the feminine form.

It's the masculine form of adjectives you'll find when you look a word up in a dictionary and, as you might expect, you often add an **-e** for the feminine form. If the masculine form of the adjective ends in a silent consonant, the extra **-e** in the feminine will cause that consonant to be sounded. (For a full pronunication guide, see page 126.)

un mot <u>français</u> *a French word*	**la langue <u>française</u>** *the French language.*
un <u>grand</u> magasin *a large shop*	**une <u>grande</u> maison** *a large house*
un <u>petit</u> village *a little village*	**une <u>petite</u> ville** *a little town*
il est <u>marié</u> *he's married*	**elle est <u>mariée</u>** *she's married*

If the masculine form already ends in an **-e** (but not **-é**), the feminine stays the same:

le vin <u>rouge</u> *red wine*	**une pomme <u>rouge</u>** *a red apple*
un musée <u>unique</u> *a unique museum*	**une maison <u>unique</u>** *a unique house*

The feminine form of some common adjectives does not follow the rules:

le vin <u>blanc</u> *white wine*	**la viande <u>blanche</u>** *white meat*
un <u>vieux</u> château *an old castle*	**une <u>vieille</u> maison** *an old house*
un <u>beau</u> pays *a beautiful country*	**une <u>belle</u> ville** *a beautiful town*
il est <u>heureux</u> *he's happy*	**elle est <u>heureuse</u>** *she's happy*
un <u>nouveau</u> restaurant *a new restaurant*	**la <u>nouvelle</u> cuisine** *(literally 'new cookery')*

Many adjectives, including colours, are placed after the thing they describe, as are longer words like **intéressant** and **internationale**: **un homme intéressant** (an interesting man), **Radio France Internationale** (International French Radio). A few very common adjectives, such as **grand**, **petit**, **vieux**, **nouveau** and **beau** are placed in front.

Prepositions

Prepositions are words like:

de of/from
dans in (a place)
à to/at (a place)
en to (a country) in (a month)
sur on
sous under
avant before
devant in front of
derrière behind

With prepositions ending in **de** or **à** such as:

à côté de next to
près de near to
en face de opposite
jusqu'à as far as

you need to note the gender of the noun that follows, as the preposition changes a little:

à côté de _la_ boulangerie next to the baker's (it's **_la_ boulangerie**)
à côté de _l'_arrêt de bus next to the bus stop (it's **_l'_arrêt**, starting with a vowel)
à côté _du_ tabac next to the tobacconist's (it's **_le_ tabac**)

jusqu'à _la_ place as far as the square (it's **_la_ place**)
jusqu'à _l'_hôtel as far as the hotel (it's **_l'_hôtel**, starting with a silent 'h')
jusqu'_au_ magasin as far as the shop (it's **_le_ magasin**)

À can be followed by **la** and **l'**, but not by **le**; in this case it becomes **au**.
De can also be followed by **la** and **l'**, but not by **le**; in this case it becomes **du**.

You

There are two ways of saying 'you' in French. **Vous** is the one you'll need when talking to strangers or casual acquaintances, including shop assistants, waiters and hotel staff, so it's the most useful form.

If you meet up with people you hit it off with, they might ask you to call them **tu** (it's more informal).

The **vous** form of a verb almost always ends in **-ez**, except for:

vous faites you do/make
vous dites you say/tell
and
vous êtes you are.

The **vous** form is also used when you're talking to more than one person.

The **tu** verb form is usually shorter than the **vous** form; when written down it nearly always ends with a (silent) **-s** or **-x**.

For regular verbs like **chercher** (to look for) the **tu** part sounds the same as the **je** part:
je cherche
tu cherches

Choosing to be formal (**vous**) or informal (**tu**) affects other words too. Look at how the word for 'your' changes in the following sentences: **Vous avez perdu <u>votre</u> sac?** **<u>Tu</u> as perdu <u>ton</u> sac?** (Have you lost your bag?).

A shorthand way of asking a question can be to make a statement: **Je m'appelle Ron** (My name is Ron) and add afterwards: **Et vous?** (How about you?). If you use the shorthand question in a friendly context, it would go like this: **Je m'appelle Ron** (My name is Ron), and afterwards: **Et toi?** (How about you?). (For more on possessive words see Gender.)

Verbs

THE INFINITIVE

In English 'I am' is part of the verb 'to be'; in French **Je suis** is part of the verb **être**. 'To be' and **être** are called infinitives.

If you are looking something up, you could ask yourself 'Which verb does this part come from?'. Your answer will be a word with 'to …' in front of it, in English – that's the word that will appear in the dictionary.

These are all infinitives – in French, infinitives often end in **-er**, **-ir** or **-re**.

lire to read
regarder to watch
dire to say
venir to come
faire to do
boire to drink

The infinitive doesn't tell you who is doing the action, nor give any indication of tense – for that, you need to take off the infinitive ending and add various sets of endings (see below).

PRESENT TENSE

'I am going' is in the present, and comes from the verb 'to go', so you look up 'go' in the dictionary and find **aller**. The part you need is **Je vais** (I am going).

There are a further five forms:

je vais I'm going
tu vas you're going (friendly)
il/elle/on va he/she is going/we're going
nous allons we're going
vous allez you're going (formal or plural)
ils/elles vont they're going

Remember **on** is used a great deal in day-to-day French instead of **nous** to mean 'we'. (It is also used to mean 'you' in a general sense.)

In English, there are two ways of talking about the present – 'I go' and 'I am going'.
In French there is only one: *je vais*.

Verbs that are regular (i.e. that follow 'a rule' – *une règle*) belong to three groups, with
their infinitives ending in either *-er*, *-ir*, or *-re*. The *-er* ending is by far the most common.

Verbs ending in -er	Verbs ending in -ir	Verbs ending in -re
Examples: **chercher** *to look for* **regarder** *to look at* **jouer** *to play*	Examples: **finir** *to finish* **choisir** *to choose*	Examples: **répondre** *to answer* **vendre** *to sell*
Take off the *-er* to get a stem (e.g. **cherch-**) and add the ending that matches	Take off the *-ir* to get a stem (e.g. **fin-**) and add the ending that matches	Take off the *-re* to get a stem (e.g. **répond-**) and add the ending that matches
je cherche	je finis	je réponds
tu cherches	tu finis	tu réponds
il/elle/on cherche	il/elle/on finit	il/elle/on répond
nous cherchons	nous finissons	nous répondons
vous cherchez	vous finissez	vous répondez
ils/elles cherchent	ils/elles finissent	ils/elles répondent

Many common verbs are irregular and do not follow these rules, although you will
notice similarities. Here are some of the most useful:

être *(to be)*

je	suis
tu	es
il/elle/on	est
nous	sommes
vous	êtes
ils/elles	sont

aller *(to go)*

je	vais
tu	vas
il/elle/on	va
nous	allons
vous	allez
ils/elles	vont

boire *(to drink)*

je	bois
tu	bois
il/elle/on	boit
nous	buvons
vous	buvez
ils/elles	boivent

avoir *(to have)*

j'	ai
tu	as
il/elle/on	a
nous	avons
vous	avez
ils/elles	ont

prendre *(to take)*

je	prends
tu	prends
il/elle/on	prend
nous	prenons
vous	prenez
ils/elles	prennent

dire *(to say)*

je	dis
tu	dis
il/elle/on	dit
nous	disons
vous	dites
ils/elles	disent

faire *(to do, make)*

je	fais
tu	fais
il/elle/on	fait
nous	faisons
vous	faites
ils	font

venir *(to come)*

je	viens
tu	viens
il/elle/on	vient
nous	venons
vous	venez
ils/elles	viennent

savoir *(to know)*

je	sais
tu	sais
il/elle/on	sait
nous	savons
vous	savez
ils/elles	savent

The next three irregular verbs are often followed by another verb in the infinitive form.

pouvoir *(to be able, 'can')*

je	peux
tu	peux
il/elle/on	peut
nous	pouvons
vous	pouvez
ils/elles	peuvent

vouloir *(to want)*

je	veux
tu	veux
il/elle/on	veut
nous	voulons
vous	voulez
ils/elles	veulent

devoir *(to have to, 'must'; to owe)*

je	dois
tu	dois
il/elle/on	doit
nous	devons
vous	devez
ils/elles	doivent

PAST TENSE (PASSÉ COMPOSÉ)

The two most useful verbs are definitely **avoir** and **être**, as they also let you talk about the past.

J'ai pris une photo. *I have taken/I took a photo.*

Je suis allé au marché ce matin. *I went/I have been to the market this morning.*

(NB. This last example catches people out more than anything else, as it looks like the English form *'I am …'*. If someone says **Je suis** followed by a part of the verb from the list below, such as **allé**, they are always talking about the past – *'I went/I have been'* and not *'I am going'*.)

The **passé composé** is composed of two parts: the auxiliary (part of **avoir** or **être**) and the past participle.

Most verbs use **avoir** as the auxiliary. The verbs that use **être** are mostly to do with movement:

aller	to go	je suis allé	I went/have been
venir	to come	je suis venu	I came/have come
arriver	to arrive	je suis arrivé	I arrived
partir	to leave	il est parti	he (has) left
sortir	to go/come out	il est sorti	he went/has gone out
entrer	to come/go in	je suis entré	I came/went in
rentrer	to go/come home	je suis rentré	I came/went home
retourner	to return	il est retourné	he returned
descendre	to go down	il est descendu	he went down(stairs)
monter	to go up	il est monté	he went up(stairs)
rester	to stay	je suis resté	I stayed
tomber	to fall down	je suis tombé	I fell
naître	to be born	il est né	he was born
mourir	to die	il est mort	he died

All the verbs that have **se** in front of them in the dictionary, for instance **se lever** *(to get up)* – **Je me suis levé** *(I got up)* – also use **être**.

For verbs that use **être**, the past participles agree in the same way as the adjectives mentioned earlier in this Toolkit. For example, they add an extra (usually silent) **-e** if it is a woman speaking, or if you are talking about a woman (**je suis alleé**, **elle est venue** etc).

All other verbs use **avoir**. Some of the common ones in the **je** form are:

j'ai acheté	I (have) bought
j'ai demandé	I (have) asked
j'ai mangé	I ate/have eaten
j'ai regardé	I (have) watched
j'ai visité	I (have) visited

j'ai choisi	I chose/have chosen
j'ai compris	I (have) understood
j'ai dit	I (have) said/told
j'ai fini	I (have) finished
j'ai mis	I (have) put
j'ai pris	I took/have taken

j'ai bu	I drank/have drunk
j'ai dû	I (have) had to
j'ai pu	I was/have been able to
j'ai voulu	I (have) wanted to
j'ai vu	I saw/have seen

j'ai fait	I made/did (have made/done)

There are other tenses to explore too ...

TALKING ABOUT THE FUTURE

As with English, French has a few ways of talking about the future, but perhaps the most simple and most useful in conversation is the one that corresponds exactly with the English:

je vais (I am going) **regarder** (to watch)

I'm going to watch the football – **Je vais regarder le football**.

To make it into 'We're going to watch' use **on**, which you've seen before: **On va regarder**. Or to ask someone, 'Are you going to watch the football?': **Vous allez/tu vas regarder le football?** (See page 122 to see how the rest of **aller** is formed.)

French also has a specific future tense, which looks very different from its English equivalent. English uses an auxiliary verb ('will' or 'shall'):

I will go
She will arrive
We shall see

French uses a very noticeable ending. All verbs in the future have the same endings, which you can hear because they have a strong **-r-** sound in them.

Here, for example, is the verb 'to visit' in the future:

English	French
Infinitive – *to visit*	Infinitive – *visiter*
I will visit	je visiter**ai**
you will visit	tu visiter**as**
he/she will visit	il/elle visiter**a**
we will visit	nous visiter**ons**
you will visit	vous visiter**ez**
they will visit	ils/elles visiter**ont**

You'll notice that the stem (ending with the **-er**) is the same as the infinitive; for verbs ending in **-ir** the same pattern applies (**je finirai**) and for those ending in **-re** the same applies again, with just the loss of the final **-e** (**je répondrai**).

The irregular verbs in the future have irregular stems, but these stems still all end in **-r**.

Three of the most common are:

j'irai I'll go (from **aller**)
je serai I'll be (from **être**)
j'aurai I'll have (from **avoir**).

Negatives

If you see or hear these words in a sentence, beware! They are negatives, which means that they completely change the sense of the rest of the sentence:

personne nobody, no-one
jamais never
rien nothing
plus no longer, no more
pas not
que only (which isn't negative in English, but is in French)

In proper written French these are matched up with the word **ne**, so you can see them coming.

Je ne sais pas. I don't know.
Je ne comprends pas. I don't understand.
Le château n'ouvre que le matin. The castle is only open in the mornings.
Je n'achète rien. I am not buying anything.
Je ne suis plus marié(e). I am not married any longer.
Vous ne mangez jamais de viande? Do you never eat meat?

You'll notice that the **ne** part of the negative is split up from the other part. The word between them is usually the verb.

In idiomatic spoken French the **ne** is often left out or not stressed enough to hear it. If it is there, it's often slurred.

J'sais (= Je ne sais) pas I dunno (don't know)

C'est (= ce n'est) pas grave It doesn't matter (lit. it's not serious)

Always use **de** (not **du, de la, de l'** or **des**) after the negative words above.

Il n'y a plus de chambres. There aren't any more rooms.

Je n'ai pas de monnaie. I haven't got any change.

Asking questions

In English, when we ask questions, there is a variety of ways of doing it, according to the subtlety of what we mean …

Sometimes, we change the word order from the basic statement form:
You are going to France → Are you going to France?
You've been to Provence before → Have you been to Provence before?

Sometimes, we add an extra word:
You go to France every year → Do you go to France every year?

Or change the words entirely:
You went to France last year → Did you go to France last year?

In French there is less variety to worry about.

The easiest way is simply to raise your voice at the end of the sentence:
Vous allez en France → **Vous allez en France?**
(You are going to France → Are you going to France?)
Vous êtes allés en France → **Vous êtes allés en France?**
(You went to France → Did you go to France?)

You could add **Est-ce que ...**:
Vous allez en France → **Est-ce que vous allez en France?**
(lit. *Is it (true) that you are going to France?*)
Vous êtes allés en France → **Est-ce que vous êtes allés en France?**
(You went to France → Did you go to France?)

You could change the word order:
Vous allez en France → **Allez-vous en France?**
(You are going to France → Are you going to France?)
Vous êtes allés en France → **Êtes-vous allés en France?**
(You went to France → Did you go to France?)

Of course, both languages also use specific question words:
Pourquoi? (Why?) **Comment?** (How?) **Quand?** (When?) **Qui?** (Who?) **Où?** (Where?)
Qu'est-ce que? (What?) **Quel(le)?** (Which?)

These can be combined with any of the word-order combinations above:
Où habitez-vous? Vous habitez où? Où est-ce que vous habitez?

All mean exactly the same thing, '*Where do you live?*', and are equally correct!

Likewise, to find out what time the train leaves you could say either:
À quelle heure part le train? or **Le train part à quelle heure?**

Pronunciation guide

In the programmes, the celebrities run into pronunciation difficulties from time to time, particularly Ron, often because he is relying on reading aloud without drilling himself on the rules of speech. For example, when he's training the team and wants them to pass the ball to the left wing, he shouts, 'Gouch!'. Sadly, 'gouch' is not a recognisable word in any language the players know. Ron was trying to say **gauche** (left).

Football commentators are not alone in having problems with mispronunciation, but their efforts are exposed to the world! Fortunately, for those of us less in the public eye, our embarrassment will not be replayed dozens of times and we can simply learn from it. As you can see from Ron's experience, the correct pronunciation of a word is as important to learn as the word itself.

The best way to acquire good pronunciation is to listen to as much French as possible and to imitate what you hear. You'll notice, among other differences, that French contains several nasal sounds not used in English, and that the *r* is rolled slightly.

The letters at the end of many French words may cause you a problem, especially if you're reading them. For instance, the *-es* and *-ent* on the end of some verb forms are silent: *(je) cherche, (tu) cherches* and *(ils) cherchent* all sound exactly the same. The *s* on the end of a plural word is also usually silent: there is no difference in how *maison* and *maisons* sound, for example. A final *t* can also be silent, as in: *le pont* (bridge), *le chat* (cat), *un avocat* (lawyer, or avocado!). However, a *-te* at the end of the word will be audible, as in: *une avocate* (female lawyer).

You will also hear liaisons, when one word flows into the next, especially where an *-s* comes before a vowel or silent 'h': *les enfants* (the children), *six heures* (6 o'clock).

You'll find your audio toolkit in the Interactive section of your DVD, in Theme 1, Audio clips. This lets you hear some key French sounds to help you build up an idea of how they are written, and what they feel like in your mouth, from the French *r* to the 'e acute'.

A word that contains each sound is also included, so when you look up a new word in your dictionary think about these basic sounds before you try to say it – sort your r's from your elbow!

Theme 1 / Section 2:8 DVD	a	avocat	ai	j'ai	an	charmant	au	au
	ail	portail	ain	maintenant	ar	départ		

Theme 1 / Section 2:9 DVD	e	le	é	thé	en	enchanté	eu	euro
	ère	portière	eil	vieille	ez	avez-vous?		

Theme 1 / Section 2:10 DVD	i	ici	in	matin	ille	fille	ien	rien

Theme 1 / Section 2:11 DVD	o	bistrot	oi	je vois	on	pont	oin	point
	ou	où	our	pour	oir	noir		

Theme 1 / Section 2:12 DVD	u	vu	un	un	une	lune		

Theme 1 / Section 2:13 DVD	-ge	voyage	-gne	champagne	-gue	mangue	-gnon	champignon
	-che	dimanche	-ce	mince				
	-the	menthe						

Theme 1 / Section 2:14 DVD	r	rare						
	w	wagon	y	il y a				

127

THEME 1

TRY IT OUT, PAGE 11

Suggested answers:
1 Il y a un parking près d'ici, s'il vous plaît?
2 Il y a un hôpital près d'ici, s'il vous plaît?
3 S'il vous plaît, il y a un cinéma près d'ici?
4 Il y a un tarif réduit pour les enfants?

TRY IT OUT, DVD ACTIVITY

Transcript:
Je travaille à la télé et dans des clubs.
J'ai deux petits enfants.
Je suis humoriste.
Je m'appelle … (Marcus).

Je travaille à la radio et à la télé.
Je suis marié.
Je suis commentateur de foot.
Je m'appelle … (Ron).

Je suis journaliste.
Je travaille à la télé.
J'ai deux filles, Emily et Rebecca.
Je m'appelle … (Esther).

Translation:
I work on television and in clubs.
I've got two small children.
I'm a comedian.
My name is … (Marcus).

I work on radio and television.
I'm married.
I'm a football commentator.
My name is … (Ron).

I'm a journalist.
I work on television.
I have two daughters, Emily and Rebecca.
My name is … (Esther).

TRY IT OUT, PAGE 15

Train + Hôtel + Voiture
Au départ de
À destination de
jour/mois/année (day/month/year)

TRY IT OUT, PAGE 20

1 Vous avez des enfants?
2 Vous avez des oranges?
3 Vous avez une voiture pour moi?

TRY IT OUT, PAGE 22

Le: téléphone/marché/cinéma/parking/journal/plan
La: voiture/piscine/photocopieuse/chambre

DVD CHALLENGE

Transcript (correct answers in bold):
J'ai Ron.
Je viens de Ron.
Je m'appelle Ron Atkinson.
Il y a un Ron Atkinson.

J'ai deux enfants.
Je viens de Londres.
J'habite près de Londres.
Je travaille à Birmingham.

Je suis mariée.
Je m'appelle Esther.
Je suis présentatrice à la télé.
Il y a un journaliste.

Il y a une piscine?
Il y a un parking près d'ici?
Il y a une boîte à lettres près d'ici?
Il y a un ascenseur?

Il y a un ascenseur ici?
Il y a une place libre?
Il y a un restaurant près d'ici?
Il y a une poubelle?

Vous avez une chambre?
Vous avez un timbre?
Vous avez une piscine?
Vous avez un hôtel?

Translation (correct answers in bold):
I have got Ron.
I come from Ron.
My name is Ron Atkinson.
There is a Ron Atkinson.

I've got two children.
I come from London.
I live near London.
I work in Birmingham.

I'm married.
My name is Esther.
I'm a TV presenter.
There is a journalist.

Is there a pool?
Is there a car park nearby?
Is there a postbox nearby?
Is there a lift?

Is there a lift here?
Is there a free seat?
Is there a restaurant near here?
Is there a bin?

Have you got a room?
Have you got a stamp?
Have you got a pool?
Have you got a hotel?

THEME 2

TRY IT OUT, PAGE 25
Suggested answers:
1 Bonjour, messieurs-dames.
2 Bonjour, monsieur.
3 (Bonjour) mademoiselle.
4 Bonjour, mesdames, comment allez-vous?

THE BIG DIFFERENCES, PAGE 25
Translation:
– Good morning.
Good morning.
– How do you do?/How are you?
Well, thank you. How about you?
– Well, thank you. Right then, see you soon.
Goodbye and have a good day.

– Hi!
Morning!
– Are you OK?
Yes, fine, and you?
– Fine, thanks.
Bye.

TRY IT OUT, DVD ACTIVITY
Transcript (correct answers in bold):
Bonjour, monsieur. Comment allez-vous?
Comment ça va?
Ça va.
Vous allez bien?
Bien, merci, et vous?

Salut, Pascale, ça va?
Oui, ça va, et toi?
Vous allez bien?
Bonne journée.
À bientôt.

Bonsoir, monsieur, je me présente. Je m'appelle Christine Montand. Voici mon compagnon Georges.
Ça va.
Enchanté.
Bonne journée.
Comment allez-vous?

Translation (correct answers in bold):
Good morning. How are you?
How are you?
All right.
Are you well?
Fine, thanks, and you?

Hi, Pascale, are things OK?
Yes, fine, and you?
Are you well?
Have a good day.
See you soon.

Good evening, may I introduce myself? My name is Christine Montand. This is my partner George.
All right.
Pleased to meet you.
Have a good day.
How are you?

THE BIG DIFFERENCES, PAGE 31
Answers:
Je suis anglaise (I'm English – female)
Je suis écossaise (I'm Scottish – female)
Je suis galloise (I'm Welsh – female)
Je suis irlandaise (I'm Irish – female)

TRY IT OUT, PAGE 33
1 Je cherche l'ascenseur.
2 Je cherche la sortie.
3 Je cherche un téléphone.
4 Je cherche ma chambre.

TRY IT OUT, PAGE 34
Suggested answers:
1 Je cherche les toilettes, s'il vous plaît.
2 Vous avez des timbres?
3 Excusez-moi, il y a une banque près d'ici?

ANSWERS

TRY IT OUT, PAGE 35

Answers:

1 The writer has a daughter of 15. They live in Provence.
2 She wants to swap houses for a fortnight in July (15 days, as they say in French). She'd prefer a house in the north of Great Britain, in a village or the countryside.
3 She has a small house – two bedrooms, bathroom, kitchen, living room, terrace and pool.

Translation of posting:

Hello everyone!
I'm looking for someone to exchange houses with this summer. I want to spend 15 days in Great Britain, preferably in the north, in a village or in the countryside, and I'd like to do a simple house swap.
I need two bedrooms – one for me and one for my daughter (15 years old). At our house in Provence, we have a little house with 2 bedrooms, bathroom, kitchen, sitting room, terrace and swimming pool.
We'd like to leave during the month of July.
Interested?
Juliette

DVD CHALLENGE

Transcript (correct answers in bold):

Bonsoir, monsieur. Vous cherchez quelque chose?
Oui, je cherche les toilettes.
Non, je cherche une table.
Non, on cherche la Place de la Concorde.
Oui, on cherche des places libres.

Ah, vous êtes touriste? Je me présente. Je m'appelle Alain.
Bonsoir. Je suis Alain.
Bonsoir, Alain. Je me présente.
Enchanté. Je m'appelle Robert.
Enchanté. Voici Robert.

Enchanté, Robert. Vous êtes anglais?
Non, je suis français.
Non, je suis écossais.
Oui, je suis anglais.
Voici une Écossaise.

Ah, très bien. Vous habitez à Édimbourg?
Non, j'habite à Dundee.
J'habite à Édimbourg.
Oui, c'est Dundee.
Je viens de Glasgow.

Vous êtes marié?
Non, je suis écossais.
Oui, voici ma femme, Emily.
Oui, voici mon mari, Emily.
C'est mon mari, Alain.

Ah, enchanté. Vous avez des enfants?
Oui, j'ai un enfant.
Oui, j'ai deux filles.
Oui, j'ai un fils et une fille.
Non, j'ai deux chiens.

Translation (correct answers in bold):

Hello, are you looking for something?
Yes, I'm looking for the toilets.
No, I'm looking for a table.
No, we're looking for the Place de la Concorde.
Yes, we're looking for some free seats.

Oh, you're a tourist? Let me introduce myself. I'm Alain.
Good evening. I'm Alain.
Good evening, Alain. Let me introduce myself.
Pleased to meet you. I'm Robert.
Pleased to meet you. This is Robert.

Pleased to meet you, Robert. Are you English?
No, I'm French.
No, I'm Scottish.
Yes, I'm English.
This is a Scotswoman.

Oh, very good. Do you live in Edinburgh?
No, I live in Dundee.
I live in Edinburgh.
Yes, it's Dundee.
I come from Glasgow.

Are you married?
No, I'm Scottish.
Yes, this is my wife, Emily.
Yes, this is my husband, Emily.
It's my husband, Alain.

Oh, pleased to meet you. Have you got any children?
Yes, I have one child.
Yes. I have two daughters.
Yes, I have one son and one daughter.
No, I have two dogs.

THEME 3

TRY IT OUT, PAGE 40

Transcript:

Il me faut du chocolat, s'il vous plaît. (D)
Un kilo de carottes, s'il vous plaît. (B)
Vous avez des oignons, s'il vous plaît? (E)
Je voudrais de la limonade. (F)
Un litre de lait, s'il vous plaît. (C)
Vous avez une bouteille d'huile d'olive? (A)

Translation:

I need some chocolate, please. (D)
A kilo of carrots, please. (B)
Do you have any onions, please? (E)
I'd like some lemonade. (F)
A litre of milk, please. (C)
Do you have a bottle of olive oil? (A)

THE BIG DIFFERENCES, PAGE 43

Je ne parle pas espagnol.
Je ne sais pas.
Je ne comprends pas.
Je n'aime pas faire les courses.
Je n'aime pas travailler ici.

TRY IT OUT, DVD ACTIVITY

Transcript:

Bonjour, madame, qu'est-ce qu'il vous faut?
– Je voudrais une bouteille d'huile d'olive, s'il vous plaît.
Oui, madame, voilà.
– Vous avez des oignons?
Non, madame, je suis désolé.

– Bien, alors, il me faut aussi du fromage.
Oui, j'ai du brie et du camembert.
– Merci, je n'aime pas le camembert. Je vais prendre un morceau de brie.

Très bien, madame, et avec ça?
– Un paquet de biscuits, s'il vous plaît. Ça fait combien?
Cinq euros, madame.
– Voilà. Je cherche un café. Est-ce qu'il y a un café près d'ici?
Oui, madame, près de la boulangerie.
– Merci, monsieur. Au revoir.
Au revoir, madame. Bonne journée!

Translation:

Good morning, what would you like?
– I'd like a bottle of olive oil, please.

Yes, there you are.
– Have you got any onions?
No, I'm sorry.

– OK, well, I also need some cheese.
Yes, I've got Brie and Camembert.
– I don't like Camembert, thank you. I'll take a slice of Brie.

Very good. Anything else?
– A packet of biscuits, please. How much is that?
€5.
– There you are. I'm looking for a café. Is there a café near here?
Yes, near the baker's.
– Thank you. Goodbye.
Goodbye. Have a nice day.

TRY IT OUT, PAGE 46

Suggested answers:

1 Un tee-shirt, c'est combien, s'il vous plaît?
2 Une bouteille d'eau minérale, c'est combien, s'il vous plaît?
3 Les melons, c'est combien, s'il vous plaît?

MAKE FRIENDS WITH YOUR DICTIONARY, PAGE 48

1 to read – *lire*
2 to watch – *regarder*
3 to need – *avoir besoin*
4 to think - *penser*
5 to say – *dire*
6 to come – *venir*
7 to do – *faire*

TRY IT OUT, PAGE 49

You could say:

1 Je peux avoir une bouteille d'eau, s'il vous plaît?
Je voudrais une bouteille d'eau, s'il vous plaît.
Il me faut une bouteille d'eau, s'il vous plaît.
Une bouteille d'eau, s'il vous plaît.

2 Je peux regarder votre magazine?
Votre magazine … je peux?
Le magazine … je peux?
Je peux …?

3 Je peux essayer ce tee-shirt?
Ce tee-shirt … je peux l'essayer?
Je peux essayer?
Je peux essayer ces baskets?
Ces baskets … je peux les essayer?
Je peux essayer?

TRY IT OUT, VIDEO CLIP, PAGE 50

Suggested answers:

Excusez-moi, est-ce que vous avez de la lotte? (Excuse me, do you have any monkfish?)

Excusez-moi, est-ce que vous avez des grenades? (Excuse me, do you have any pomegranates?)

TRY IT OUT, PAGE 53

Order of prices:

€1.80
€6.75
€18.10
€1.20
€4.90
€20
€8.70
€5.50

VIDEO CLIP 2, PAGE 53

Answers:

1 between 26 and 60 years old
2 65 years old
3 between 3 and 8pm

Transcript:

Esther: Bonjour, monsieur. Je dois aller à l'île de Porquerolles.
Man: Vous avez entre vingt-six et soixante ans? Quel âge … vous avez entre vingt-six et soixante ans?
Esther: Non, j'ai soixante-cinq ans.
Man: Donc vous avez une réduction senior.
Esther: C'est bien.
Man: Ah non … pas sur ce train parce qu'on est vendredi entre quinze et vingt heures.

Translation:

Esther: Hello. I need to get to the island of Porquerolles.
Man: Are you between 26 and 60 years old? How old… are you between 26 and 60 years old?
Esther: No, I'm 65 years old.
Man: In that case there is a pensioner's reduction.
Esther: That's great.
Man: Actually … not on this train because it's between 3 and 8pm on a Friday.

MARCEL'S ONION SOUP, PAGE 56

Translation:

To make onion soup for 5 people
1 kilo of onions
a little butter or oil
flour (2 soupspoons)
dry white wine (½ litre)

chicken or beef stock (2 litres)
salt and pepper
1 dry baguette
250g grated cheese (preferably Gruyère)

• fry the onions lightly in the butter or oil until just golden
• liquidise
• add the flour and mix together
• stir slowly with the white wine added, over a low heat (add salt and pepper if necessary)
• make 2 litres of stock and stir into the onions, heat gently for half an hour – this is the liquid part of the soup
• cut the bread into thin slices and grill until lightly toasted
• take a deep dish, and put on the bottom a layer of toast, followed by a layer of cheese
• add some of the liquid till moist
• then add another layer of toast, followed by a layer of cheese, and pour more liquid over the top to moisten
• put in the oven to grill the top – this is the 'croûtons' part of the soup.
• to serve the soup, put some of the croûtons part into the dish, followed by some of the liquid part

MAKE FRIENDS WITH YOUR DICTIONARY, PAGE 58

Answers:

recruter – to recruit
finir – to finish
préparer – to prepare
tour – tour
cool – cool
intéressant – interesting
cultivés – cultivated

Transcript:

Thierry: OK Esther, maintenant vous êtes seule. Vous avez jusqu'à dix-sept heures pour recruter les clients […] et finir de préparer votre tour pour demain. […]
Esther: C'est cool, c'est intéressant … et vous êtes des gens très cultivés.

Translation:

Thierry: OK Esther, now you're on your own. You have got until 5 o'clock to recruit your clients […] and to finish preparing your tour for tomorrow. […]
Esther: It's cool, it's interesting … and you're such cultured people .

DVD CHALLENGE

Transcript (model answers in bold):

Bonjour madame, vous désirez?
Je voudrais un tee-shirt.

Oui. Quelle taille?
Quarante.
Très bien. Quelle couleur?
Vous avez ce tee-shirt en rose?
Non, madame, je l'ai en blanc, bleu et orange.
C'est combien, un tee-shirt?
Trois euros cinquante.
Trois euros cinquante. C'est ça?
Oui, madame, c'est ça.
Je vais prendre le bleu, s'il vous plaît.

Translation (model answers in bold):
Good morning, what would you like?
I'd like a T-shirt.
Yes, what size?
40.
OK. What colour?
Have you got this T-shirt in pink?
No, I've got it in white, blue and orange.
How much is a T-shirt?
€3.50.
€3.50, is that right?
Yes, that's right.
I'll take the blue one, please.

THEME 4

TRY IT OUT, PAGE 62

You can pick the version you like best, but you could say:

1 S'il vous plaît, on cherche la station-service. (Please, we're looking for the petrol station.)
Il y a une station-service près d'ici, s'il vous plaît? (Is there a petrol station near here, please?)
J'ai besoin de trouver une station-service, s'il vous plaît. (I need to find a petrol station, please.)

2 Pour aller à la place de la mairie, s'il vous plaît? (How do I get to the town hall square, please?)
Je cherche la mairie, s'il vous plaît. (I'm looking for the town hall, please.)
Je suis désolé, je ne trouve pas la mairie. (I'm sorry; I can't find the town hall.)

3 Pour le parking, s'il vous plaît. (I need the car park, please.)
Je cherche le parking, s'il vous plaît. (I'm looking for the car park, please.)
Savez-vous où se trouve le parking? (Do you know where the car park is?)

4 Je cherche la rue de Grenoble, s'il vous plaît. (I'm looking for Grenoble Street, please.)
La rue de Grenoble, s'il vous plaît. (Grenoble Street, please.)
Où se trouve la rue de Grenoble, s'il vous plaît? (Where is Grenoble Street, please?)

TRY IT OUT, PAGE 64

Suggested answers:

1 Excusez-moi. La rue est à sens unique? (Excuse me, is this a one-way street?)
2 Il y a des travaux? (Are there any roadworks?)
3 Je voudrais un plan, s'il vous plaît. (I'd like a town map, please.)

There are several ways of phrasing things, of course:

4 C'est pour un renseignement. Je peux stationner ici? (I need some information. Can I park here?) Or Il y a un parking ici? (Is there a car park here?)

TRY IT OUT, PAGE 65

Suggested answers:

1 Pouvez-vous m'indiquer la route pour Aix-en-Provence?
2 Pouvez-vous me dire, qu'est-ce que c'est?
3 Pouvez-vous parler plus lentement?
4 Pouvez-vous me recommander un restaurant?

TRY IT OUT, DVD ACTIVITY

Transcript:

Pouvez-vous me recommander un hôtel près de l'Arc de Triomphe, s'il vous plaît?

J'ai besoin d'un renseignement. Savez-vous où je peux acheter des olives, s'il vous plaît?

Excusez-moi, monsieur. Vous pouvez me dire … je peux stationner ici?

Translation:

Could you recommend a hotel near the Arc de Triomphe, please?

I need some information. Do you know where I can buy olives, please?

Excuse me, sir. Can you tell me … can I park here?

TRY IT OUT, SPELLING PRACTICE, PAGE 68

Saint-Rémy
Marseille
Cannes
Hyères

Montpellier
Agde
Béziers
Les Baux
Carcassonne

TRY IT OUT, TOWN PLAN, PAGE 72

Answers:
1 L'office du tourisme = no 3
2 La gare = no 12
3 L'Hôtel St Georges = no 5

Translation:
1 For the tourist office, go down rue de la Comédie, pass in front of the town hall and turn right at the square. It's there, on your right.
2 For the station, take avenue Colbert. Go straight on until the lights. You'll see the station on your left.
3 For the Hotel St Georges, take avenue Colbert. Go straight on until the lights. You'll see the station on your left. Carry straight on and then turn left again.

THE BIG DIFFERENCES, PAGE 73

1 Pour aller à la station-service?
2 Pour aller au marché?
3 Pour aller à l'office du tourisme?
4 Pour aller au restaurant Chez Nico?
5 Pour aller à Miramas?
6 Pour aller à la boulangerie?

TRY IT OUT, PAGE 74

Transcript:
Esther: Quatre personnes, deux enfants, période bleue, quatre bicyclettes. Un homme qui visite ma maison … tout ça.

Translation:
Esther: Four people, two children, blue period, four bicycles. A man who's visiting my house … all that.

TRY IT OUT, PAGE 75

Answer:
Marcus says: Je ne sais pas le mot 'ours' (I don't know the word 'ours'). In fact, to be strictly correct, Marcus should have used: Je ne connais pas ('I don't know' in the sense 'I'm not familiar' with) but his audience still understood.

Transcript:
Marcus: Est-ce que vous tous, marseillaises? Non? Qui dit non? […] Oui? Où habitez-vous, monsieur?
Man: Dans la montagne.
Marcus: Dans la montagne!

Man: Les Pyrénées.
Marcus: Et monsieur, dans les montagnes … qu'est-ce que vous faites?
Man: Je cherche des ours.
Marcus: Chercher les …?
Man: Les ours.
Marcus: Oui, bien. *Je ne sais pas le mot 'ours'*. C'est pas grave, je crois qu'il est un …
Audience: Bear!
Marcus: 'Bear'? Oui? Bien! Voilà, la barbe! C'est très important pour les bears. Vous restez dans les arbres avec la barbe … et le bear dit "Ah! Maman!".

Transcript:
Marcus: Is it you all, from Marseilles? No? Who says no? Yes? Where do you live?
Man: In the mountains.
Marcus: In the mountains!
Man: The Pyrenees.
Marcus: And in the mountains … what do you do?
Man: I look for bears.
Marcus: Look for …?
Man: Bears.
Marcus: Yes, good. I know not the word 'bears'. It doesn't matter, I think he's a …
Audience: Bear!
Marcus: Ah, the beard! It's very important for the bears. You stay in the trees with the beard … and the bear says "Oh, Mummy!"

TRY IT OUT, PAGE 76

Suggested answers:
1 Bonjour. Il me faut un aller simple, première classe, non-fumeur, pour Nice, s'il vous plaît.
2 Un aller-retour pour Toulouse, en seconde, s'il vous plaît.
3 Un aller simple pour Nice, pour aujourd'hui, s'il vous plaît.
4 S'il vous plaît, je voudrais un aller simple, première classe, pour Nice, pour demain.
5 C'est combien?

WORD ON THE STREET, PAGE 77

Entrée – Way in
Toilettes – Toilets
Contrôle des passeports – Passport control
Point de rencontre – Meeting (encounter) point
Départ immédiat – Immediate departure

DVD CHALLENGE

Transcript (model answers in bold):

Bonjour, madame.

Je voudrais deux aller-retours pour Biarritz.

Oui. C'est pour aujourd'hui?

Oui, c'est pour cet après-midi. C'est combien?

C'est trente-cinq euros.

Merci. Le bus part à quelle heure?

À quatorze heures trente.

Vous pouvez répéter, s'il vous plaît?

À quatorze heures trente.

Merci. Le bus part d'où, s'il vous plaît?

Du quai numéro cinq.

Où se trouve le quai numéro cinq, s'il vous plaît?

Translation (model answers in bold):

Hello madam.

I'd like two return tickets for Biarritz.

Yes. Is it for today?

Yes, it's for this afternoon. How much is it?

It's €35.

Thank you. What time does the bus leave?

At 2.30pm.

Can you repeat that please?

At 2.30pm.

Thank you. Where does the bus leave from?

From bay 5.

Where is bay 5?

THEME 5

TRY IT OUT, PAGE 82

1 Je peux avoir une liste des restaurants, s'il vous plaît?
2 Est-ce qu'il y a un camping?
3 Je voudrais un dépliant en anglais, s'il vous plaît.
4 Est-ce qu'il y a un endroit pour se promener?
5 À quelle heure ferme le parc?

TRY IT OUT, DVD ACTIVITY

S'il vous plaît, le musée est ouvert à quelle heure aujourd'hui?
– Entre dix et dix-neuf heures, monsieur.

Est-ce qu'il y a une piscine ici?
– Oui, madame. Elle est ouverte entre huit heures et midi tous les jours.

Le concert est à quelle heure?
– À vingt et une heures, monsieur.

Translation:

Excuse me, what time is the museum open today?
– Between 10am and 7pm.

Is there a pool here?
– Yes. It's open between 8am and midday every day.

What time is the concert?
– At 9pm.

TRY IT OUT, PAGE 85

Suggested answers:

1 Je vais visiter un musée cet après-midi.
2 On va aller à un concert demain.
3 On va voir une exposition ce soir.

VIDEO CLIP 1, PAGE 85

Transcript, future expressions in italics:

Florence: Donc, *tu vas aller interviewer* des gens, comme on dit en France des 'messieurs tout le monde', et *tu vas leur demander* qu'est-ce qu'ils en pensent des anglais qui s'installent dans la région. La vie rêvée des Anglais, par exemple: Peter Mayle.

Translation:

Florence: So, *you are going to interview* people, as we say in France 'Mr Average', and *you are going to ask* them what they think of the English who come and live in our area. Living the dream, like Peter Mayle.

TRY IT OUT, PAGE 87

Suggested answers:

1 Vous allez au match?
2 Tu vas au cinéma?
3 Tu as de l'argent?
4 Oui, j'ai 20 euros.
5 Vous êtes en vacances ?
6 Tu es fatigué?

TRY IT OUT, PAGE 88

Main fêtes you might have spotted:
musique, danses, histoire, littérature (music, dances, history, literature)
Dates and specific events:
début décembre (beginning of December) concert de Noël (Christmas concert)
avril (April) Festival du Tambourin (Tambourin Festival)
dernier dimanche d'avril (last Sunday in April) ascension de la montagne Sainte Victoire (ascent of the Sainte Victoire mountain)
mi-septembre (mid-September) Fête Mistralienne (Mistral Festival)

Translation of web page:

The cultural activities in Provence are part of a long and proud tradition: its music, dance, history and literature can be discovered through the special events organised in Aix-en-Provence. For example:
• Beginning of December: the Académie du Tambourin's Christmas concert.
• In April, the Provençal Tambourin festival: a competition of traditional dances and concerts.
• The 'Roumavàgi de Sainte Victoire', or the ascent of the Sainte Victoire mountain, takes place on the last Sunday in April. A mass with Provençal chants at the Chapel of the Priory, a blessing of the mountain and of the Aix area, traditional dances and music.
• In mid-September the 'Fête Mistralienne' takes place in the Parc Jourdan. Leaving from the town hall, groups of musicians and dancers parade through the park, ending up around the statue of the 'Mistral'.

EATING OUT, PAGE 89

Answers:

1 There is an *à la carte* menu and a daily specials board.
2 They ask what is on offer as they don't eat meat.
3 He offers pasta, salads, quiches and omelettes.
4 They ask what it is.
5 They choose avocado salad, tagliatelle pasta and asparagus quiche.

Translation:

– Good evening.
Good evening.
– I've reserved a table for three people, in the name of Lewis.
Of course. Follow me … Here's the menu, the dishes of the day are displayed here.
– Excuse me. I need some advice. We don't eat meat; what do you recommend?
You have a choice, there's pasta, salads, quiches and omelettes, if you like.
– And 'la bourride', what's that?
It's a typical fish dish.
– Thank you. We'll have an avocado salad, some tagliatelle … and for me … erm … I don't know … an asparagus quiche.
And to drink?
– A jug of water.
Mineral water?
– No thanks, just tap water.
OK.

VIDEO CLIP 2, PAGE 90

Answer:

She checks by repeating: C'est pas très chaud? then by re-wording: C'est froid? and by using a checking strategy: Vraiment?

Transcript:

Man: La nourriture n'est pas très chaude.
Esther: C'est pas très chaude? C'est froid? Vraiment?

Translation:

Man: The food isn't very hot.
Esther: It's not very hot? It's cold? Really?

Answer:

The chef is really annoyed; the plates were not picked up and served quickly enough.

Transcript:

Esther: Il y a des gens qui disent que les assiettes sont chaudes, mais la nourriture, c'est pas chaud.
Chef: C'est pas ma faute ça! Montrez. Mais oui, c'est froid. Il faut les enlever depuis le temps où je vous demande de l'enlever. C'est quelle table?

Translation:

Esther: Some people are saying that their plates are hot, but the food isn't.
Chef: It's not my fault! Show me. Well yes, it's cold. You're supposed to take them when I say to. Which table is it?

TRY IT OUT, PAGE 94

Answers:

1 'Est-ce que vous pouvez goûter pour moi une spécialité anglaise?'
2 There's a mixed response. Generally not very keen.
3 'Dégueulasse' is a very expressive indication of disapproval. Gross! Within the one word it sums up the message 'This makes me feel like throwing up!' Use with care!

Transcript:

Esther: Est-ce que vous pouvez goûter pour moi une spécialité anglaise?
Réponses: Je vais l'essayer, madame … Dégueulasse! […] Pauvre […] Non, c'est très bon […] Ça donne les hémorroïdes.

Translation:

Esther: Could you try an English speciality for me?
Responses: I'll try it … Disgusting! […] Poor […] No, it's very good. […] It'll give you piles.

THE BIG DIFFERENCES, PAGE 95

1 Je ne comprends rien.
2 Vous n'aimez rien?
3 Je n'ai plus d'argent.
4 Je ne fume plus.
5 Je ne travaille jamais le week-end.

TRY IT OUT, PAGE 96

Translation:

to disconnect
to discourage
to discover
to disapprove
disadvantage
to disinfect

interest (deposit)
clothes (vestments)
feast, festival
hospital
conquest
ancestor
forest

disgusting
destroyed
oysters

DVD CHALLENGE

Transcript (model answers in bold):

Tu es libre ce week-end? Vendredi ou samedi soir?
Je suis libre vendredi soir. Samedi, je vais aller à un concert.
Très bien. Vendredi, c'est bon. Tu veux aller au cinéma, ou tu préfères le théâtre?
Je voudrais aller au cinéma. J'aime le théâtre, mais je préfère le cinéma.
Super! On peut aller au multiplex. Il y a beaucoup de films – un grand choix. Tu veux aller manger avant le film?
Oui, mais je suis végétarienne – je ne mange pas de viande.
Qu'est-ce que tu manges alors?
Je mange du poisson, des pâtes, des omelettes ...
Pas de problème. Alors, on va manger à quelle heure vendredi ? Six heures? Six heures et demie?
Six heures et quart, c'est possible?
Oui, bien sûr. Alors, six heures et quart, devant la mairie. Je vais téléphoner au cinéma cet après-midi.
Très bien. Vendredi, six heures et quart, devant la mairie. À bientôt.

Translation (model answers in bold):

Are you free this weekend? Friday or Saturday evening?
I'm free on Friday evening. On Saturday I'm going to go to a concert.
Great. Friday is good. Would you like to go to the cinema, or do you prefer the theatre?
I'd like to go to the cinema. I like the theatre, but I prefer the cinema.
Great! We can go to the multiplex. There are a lot of films – a big choice. Would you like to go and eat before the film?
Yes, but I'm a vegetarian and I don't eat meat.
What do you eat then?
I eat fish, pasta, omelettes ...
No problem. Right, what time on Friday evening shall we eat? 6pm? 6.30pm?
Is 6.15pm possible?
Yes, of course. OK, 6.15pm, in front of the town hall. I'll phone the cinema this afternoon.
Fine. Friday, 6.15pm, in front of the town hall. See you soon.

THEME 6

TRY IT OUT, PAGE 99

1 Je peux emprunter une serviette?
2 Je peux prendre cette place?
3 Je peux prendre un verre d'eau?
4 Je peux prendre une photo?
5 Je peux vous apporter ça?
6 Je peux avoir celui-là/celle-là?

VIDEO CLIP 1, PAGE 102

Answers:

She toasts him by saying: Santé! (Cheers!)
She describes the pastis as good: C'est bon.

Transcript:

Michel: C'est pas vrai! Vous n'avez jamais bu de la tisane provençale?
Esther: Non. La tisane provençale! ... Santé! ... C'est bon.
Michel: Oui, c'est bon! C'est trop bon!
Esther: Il y a peut-être un danger ici ...
Michel: Oui, de trop boire, non?
Esther: Parce que pour comparer, il faut prendre un goût – est-ce qu'on dit? – et puis un autre goût ... et un autre goût! Après ça on ne peut pas discerner rien.
Michel: C'est vrai que les goûts s'annulent.

Translation:

Michel: I can't believe it! You have never tried Provençal 'tea'?

Esther: No. Provençal 'tea'! ... Cheers! ... It's good!

Michel: Yes, it's good! It's really good!

Esther: There is perhaps a danger here ...

Michel: Yes, drinking too much?

Esther: Because in order to compare you need to have a taste – do you say? – and then another taste ... and another taste! After that you can't distinguish anything.

Michel: It's true that the tastes cancel each other out.

THE CHAT, PAGE 103

She begins by taking the initiative: *Alors, j'ai préparé quelques cadeaux pour vous* (I've prepared some gifts for you) and then uses the individual gifts to steer the interview, by having a comment ready for each.

- the rose of England (the Queen)
- English food: *Je sais que notre nourriture n'est pas merveilleuse* (I know that our food isn't brilliant) leads into her question: *Est-ce que vous aimez la nourriture anglaise?* (Do you like English food?)
- she then contrasts with the toilet paper: *mais notre plomberie, c'est formidable* (but our plumbing is magnificent)

Once on a roll, Esther follows up one question (on food), which elicits a reply about liking pies, with another in simple effective words, seeking more detail: *Pies – quelle sorte?* (What sort of pies?)

Her final question is complex, about attitudes to sex scandals in politics, but Esther organises it into manageable lumps: *En Angleterre* (In England) *il y a beaucoup de journaux* (there are lots of newspapers) *qui s'occupent de* (that deal with) *la vie privée des politiciens* (the private life of politicians). *Est-ce que vous croyez* (Do you think) *que c'est une bonne idée?* (that's a good idea?)

THE BIG DIFFERENCES, PAGE 105

1 Où avez-vous dîné hier soir? or Vous avez dîné où hier soir?
2 Qu'est-ce que vous avez mangé au restaurant?
3 Pourquoi avez-vous choisi ce restaurant?

TRY IT OUT, PAGE 106

She asks 'Qu'est-ce que vous pensez des anglais?' (What do you think of the English?)

The correct question was 'Qu'est-ce que vous pensez des anglais qui s'installent dans la région?' (What do you think of the English who come and live in the area?)

Suggested answers:

1 Qu'est-ce que vous pensez du match de football?
2 Qu'est-ce que vous pensez du concert?
3 Qu'est-ce que vous pensez du vin?
4 Qu'est-ce que vous pensez du restaurant?

JOKE, PAGE 107

Translation:

People are watching the Paris Saint-Germain–Olympique Marseille match on the big screen in a bar. This guy is sitting right in front of the screen with his dog, drinking his pastis; the dog is staring at the screen.

When PSG get possession and move forward the dog gets up and starts to bark ... the closer PSG get to the goal the more he barks. When the Paris player loses the ball the dog sits down and goes quiet again.

The barman says to the guy: 'What a great dog! What does he do when they score?' He replies: 'I don't know; I've only had him six months.'

TRY IT OUT, PAGE 114

Phone numbers as words:

Zéro quatre – soixante-quatorze – vingt-sept – quarante-six – quatre-vingt-dix-neuf

Zéro trois – zéro quatre – cinquante-cinq – vingt-trois – soixante-dix-huit

Zéro deux - soixante-quatre - trente-trois - soixante-six – douze

TRY IT OUT, DVD ACTIVITY

Transcript:

Bonjour. Tous nos standardistes sont occupés. Vous pouvez nous contacter aussi au 01-74-11-38-05 ou laisser un message après le bip sonore. Merci.

Ici la messagerie vocale de Bertrand Carré. Vous pouvez laisser un message ou me contacter au numéro 06-23-78-09-53.

Vous pouvez nous contacter par téléphone en composant le numéro suivant: 01-92-63-16-28, suivi du code 96, du lundi au vendredi, de 14h à 19h.

Translation:

Hello. All our operators are busy. You can also contact us on 01-74-11-38-05, or leave a message after the tone. Thank you.

This is the voice mail of Bertrand Carré. You can leave a message or contact me on 06-23-78-09-53.

You can contact us by telephone by dialling the following number: 01-92-63-16-28, followed by code 96, from Monday to Friday from 2-7pm.

DVD CHALLENGE

Transcript (correct answers in bold):

Non, mais j'ai passé une semaine au pays de Galles.
Quand y êtes-vous allé?
Vous avez visité l'Angleterre?
Où êtes-vous allé?
Qu'est-ce que vous avez fait?

Je suis allé dans le nord et à l'île d'Anglesey. C'est un pays magnifique.
Où êtes-vous allé?
Quand y êtes-vous allé?
Avec qui êtes-vous allé?
Comment êtes-vous allé?

Parce que j'adore la montagne et les vieux châteaux.
Vous avez aimé le pays?
Qu'est-ce que vous avez fait?
Que pensez-vous du pays?
Pourquoi avez-vous aimé le pays de Galles?

Ils sont très sympathiques.
Où sont les Gallois?
Comment avez-vous trouvé les Gallois?
Pourquoi avez-vous aimé le pays de Galles?
Que pensez-vous du pays de Galles?

Oui, j'ai mangé du 'laverbread'.
Qu'est-ce que vous avez mangé?
Que pensez-vous de la cuisine?
Vous avez goûté des spécialités galloises?
Où avez-vous mangé?

C'est dégueulasse!
Où avez-vous mangé?
Qui a mangé ça?
Comment sont-ils?
Qu'est-ce que vous en pensez?

Un peu. Maintenant je connais deux ou trois mots.
Que pensez-vous de la langue galloise?
Vous avez appris la langue galloise?
Qu'est-ce que vous avez fait ?
Qui parle gallois?

Translation (correct answers in bold):

No, but I spent a week in Wales.
When did you go there?
Have you visited England?
Where did you go?
What did you do?

I went to the north and to Anglesey island. It's a wonderful country.
Where did you go?
When did you go there?
Who did you go with?
How did you go?

Because I love mountains and old castles.
Did you like the country?
What did you do?
What did you think of the country?
Why did you like Wales?

They are very nice.
Where are the Welsh?
How did you find the Welsh?
Why did you like Wales?
What did you think of Wales?

Yes, I ate 'laverbread'.
What did you eat?
What did you think of the food?
Did you taste some Welsh specialities?
Where did you eat?

It's disgusting!
Where did you eat?
Who ate that?
What are they like?
What did you think of it?

A bit. Now I know two or three words.
What do you think of the Welsh language?
Did you learn Welsh?
What did you do?
Who speaks Welsh?

This glossary contains all the words and phrases, and their meanings, as they occur in this book. Verbs are given in the form in which they occur, usually followed by the infinitive in brackets.

*	irregular verb
v.	verb
(m)	masculine
(f)	feminine
(plur)	plural
(sing)	singular

A

à to/in/at/with
à (dix) minutes (ten) minutes away
(il/elle/on) a (v. *avoir) (he/she/it) has/(we) have
à bientôt see you soon
à côté de next to
à destination de to
à droite (de) right/on the right/to the right (of)
à gauche (de) left/on the left/to the left (of)
à l' (in front of a vowel – sing) to/in/at/with
à la (+ f sing) to/in/at/with
à la campagne in the country
à la maison at home
à la vôtre! cheers!/to yours!
à tout de suite! see you very soon! (i.e. see you straight away)
à votre santé! your health!/cheers!
(il) aboie (v. *aboyer) (it) barks
(l'/la) abonné(e) (m/f) member
*aboyer to bark
l' académie (f) academy
l' accueil (m) welcome desk
accueillant(e) hospitable
(il/elle) accueille (v. *accueillir) (he/she) welcomes
*accueillir to welcome
(j') achète (v. acheter) (I) buy
acheter to buy
l' activité (f) activity
(j') adore (v. adorer) (I) love
adorer to love
l' adulte (m/f) adult
affiché(e) displayed/on display
(j') ai (v. *avoir) (I) have
aider to help
l' ail (m) garlic
(j'/il/elle) aime (v. aimer) (I/it/he/she) like(s)
aimé (v. aimer) liked
aimer to like/to enjoy
(vous) aimez (v. aimer) (you) like
ajouter to add

(vous) ajoutez (v. ajouter) (you) add
allé (v. *aller) been/gone
l' allée (f) lane/path/avenue
aller to go
l' aller simple (m) one way (ticket)
l' allergie (f) allergy
allergique (m/f) à allergic to
l' aller-retour (m) return (ticket)
allez! (v. *aller) right then!
(vous) allez (v. *aller) (you) go/are going
allez-y (v. *aller) go ahead
allô hello (on the phone)
alors then
alors? so/well/right?
l' ambiance (f) ambience
l' an (m) year
l' analyste (m/f) analyst
l' ancêtre (m) ancestor
l' anglais English (language)
l' Anglais(e) Englishman/woman
anglais(e) English
l' Angleterre (f) England
l' année (f) year
l' anniversaire (m) birthday
anticonstitutionnellement anti-constitutionally
les antiquités (f plur) antiques
l' apéritif (m) aperitif
l' apéro (m) short for apéritif
s' appeler to be called
(je) m' appelle (v. *s'appeler) (I) am called, my name is
apporter to carry
appris (v. *apprendre) learned
(il/elle) s' approche (v. s'approcher) (he/she/it) gets nearer
s' approcher to get nearer
*appuyer to press
après after
l' après-midi (m or f) afternoon
l' argent (m) money
l' arrêt (m) stop
(j') arrive à (v. arriver à) (I) manage to
arriver à (faire) to manage to (do)
(tu) as (v. *avoir) (you) have (informal)
l' ascenseur (m) lift
l' ascension (f) ascent
l' asperge (f) asparagus
s' *asseoir to sit down
(ils/elles) s'assied (v. *s'asseoir) (he/she/it) sits down
l' assiette (f) plate
assis (v. *s'asseoir) seated/sitting
l' attente (f) wait
au (= à + le) (+ m sing) to/in/at/with
au nom de in the name of
au coin at the corner
au revoir goodbye
aujourd'hui today

aussi as well/too
authentique *(m/f)* authentic
autour around
autre other
aux (= à + les) *(+ plur)* at the/to the/with
l' auxiliaire *(m)* auxiliary
l' avance *(f)* advance
avant before
avec with
avec ça? anything else?
l' avenue *(f)* avenue
(vous) avez *(v. *avoir)* (you) have
avez-vous …? have you got …?/do you have …?
l' avocat *(m)* avocado
l' avocat(e) lawyer
*avoir to have
*avoir (trente) ans to be (thirty)
*avoir besoin de to need
*avoir faim to be hungry
*avoir mal to have a pain
avril April

B

les bagages *(m plur)* luggage
la baguette French stick
se baigner to go for a swim
le bain bath
le ballon (foot)ball
la banque bank
le bar bar
le barman barman
les baskets *(m plur)* trainers
le bateau boat
beau *(m)*/bel *(m before a vowel or silent 'h')*/belle *(f)*/
beaux *(m plur)*/belles *(f plur)* beautiful/nice
la beauté beauty
beaux see *beau*
bel see *beau*
belle see *beau*
la belle-mère mother-in-law
belles see *beau*
ben! well!
la bénédiction blessing
le besoin need
le beurre butter
la bibliothèque library
la bicyclette bicycle
bien fine
bien aimer to enjoy
bien mûr(e) nice and ripe
la bière beer
le billet ticket
le bip sonore tone *(on answering machine)*
le biscuit biscuit

le bistrot bistro/café
blanc/blanche white
blanche see *blanc*
bleu clair light blue
bleu(e) blue
bleue see *bleu*
le bocal jar
le bœuf beef
*boire to drink
*boire un coup to have a drink *(informal)*
la boisson drink/beverage
(il/elle) boit *(v. *boire)* (he/she/it) drinks
la boîte box/tin
la boîte à/aux lettres letter box
bon voyage! have a good journey!
bon(ne) good
le bonbon sweet
bonjour! (good) morning!/(good) afternoon/hello!
bonne see *bon*
bonne chance! good luck!
bonne journée! have a nice day!
bonne santé! (to your) good health!
bonne soirée! have a nice evening!
bonsoir! good evening!
la boucherie butcher's
la bouillabaisse fish stew *(speciality of Marseille)*
le bouillon stock
la boulangerie baker's
la boule scoop
le boulevard boulevard
la bourride fish dish
le bout end
la bouteille bottle
le brie Brie
britannique *(m/f)* British
bu *(v. *boire)* drunk
le bureau office
le bus bus
le buste bust
le but goal

C

c'est bien ça? is this it?
c'est bien ici? am I in the right place?
c'est bien …? is it …?
ça that/that thing there
ça fait *(v. *faire)* it comes to (total)
ça fait combien? *(v. *faire)* how much is that?/how much
does that come to?
ça va *(v. *aller)* OK
ça va bien? *(see *aller)* are you OK?
ça vous intéresse? are you interested?
le cadeau present
le café coffee/café

(il/elle) se **calme** (v. se calmer) (he/she/it) calms down

se **calmer** to calm down

le **camembert** Camembert

la **campagne** countryside

le **canard** duck

la **carafe d'eau** jug of water

la **carotte** carrot

la **carte** card/menu

la **carte des boissons** drinks list

cassé(e) broken

ce sera tout? (v. *être) will that be all?

ce sont (v. *être) these are

ce (m)/**cette** (f)/**cet** (m before a vowel) this (before a noun)

celle-là see celui-là

celui-là (m)/**celle-là** (f)/**ceux-là** (m plur)/**celles-là** (f plur) that one, those ones

cent hundred

la **cerise** cherry

c'est (v. *être) it is

c'est ...? (v. *être) is it ...?

c'est-à-dire well, I mean ...

c'est bon that's OK

c'est ça that's right

c'est ça? is that right?

c'est combien? (v. *être) how much is it?/how much are they?

c'est de la part de qui? who is calling? (on the phone)

c'est quoi ...? what is ...?

cet see ce

cette see ce

la **chambre** bedroom

le **champagne** Champagne

le **champignon** mushroom

le/la **champion/ne** champion

la **chance** luck

la **chanson** song

le **chant** song

la **chapelle** chapel

la **charcuterie** delicatessen

charmant(e) charming

charmante see charmant

chasser to hunt

le **chasseur** hunter

le/les **château/châteaux** (plur) castle(s)

châteaux see château

chaud(e) hot

chaude see chaud

chauffer to heat

(vous) **chauffez** (v. chauffer) (you) heat

la **chaussure** shoe

les **chaussures** (f plur) **de plage** beach shoes

le **chef** chef

cher/chère expensive

(je/il/elle/ **cherche** (v. chercher) (I/he/she/we) am/is/are looking for
on)

(ils/elles) **cherchent** (they) are looking for

chercher to look for

(tu) **cherches** (v. chercher) (you) are looking for (informal)

(vous) **cherchez** (v. chercher) (you) are looking for (formal)

(nous) **cherchons** (we) are looking for

chère see cher

chez at someone's place

chez nous at (our) home

le **chien** dog

le/la **Chinois(e)** Chinese man/woman

les **chips** (f plur) crisps

le **chocolat** chocolate

choisi (v. choisir) chosen

le **choix** choice

ciao! bye!

le **cinéma** cinema

cinglé(e) crazy

cinq five

cinquante fifty

cinquante-cinq fifty five

cinquante-deux fifty two

clair(e) light

claire see clair

la **classe** class

le **club** club

le **code** code

coin corner

combien (de) ... how much/how many ...

combien je vous dois? (v. *devoir) how much do I owe you?

comme as/in the way of

comment how

comment? how?/pardon?

comment allez-vous? how do you do?/how are you?

comment ça s'écrit? (v. *s'écrire) how do you spell (write) it?

comment ça va? how's it going?

le **commentateur** commentator

le **commentateur de foot** football commentator

la **communication** communication

le/la **compagnon/compagne** partner

composer to dial

composter to stamp/to validate

le **composteur** stamping machine

***comprendre** to understand

(je) **comprends** (v. *comprendre) (I) understand

compris (v. *comprendre) understood

le **concert** concert

le **concours** competition

(je) **connais** (v. *connaître) (I) know

la **connaissance** acquaintance

(vous) **connaissez?** (v. *connaître) do (you) know (it)?

la **conquête** conquest

le **conseil** (a piece of) advice

(il/elle) **conserve** (v. conserver) (he/she/it) keeps/retains

conserver to keep/to retain
la consigne left luggage
consulter to consult
contacter to contact
continuer to carry on
(vous) continuez (v. continuer) (you) carry on
contre versus/against
le contrôle control
cool cool
la corniche coastal road
le cou neck
la couche layer
la couleur colour
le coup de main helping hand
couper to cut
(vous) coupez (v. couper) (you) cut
les courses (f plur) shopping
le couteau knife
le couvert place (at the table)
la crémerie dairy shop
creuse see creux
creux/euse hollow/deep
*croire to think/to believe
(je) crois (v. *croire) (I) think
le croûton croûton
cru(e) raw
crue see cru
la cuillère spoon/spoonful
la cuillère à soupe soup spoon
la cuisine kitchen/food
cuit(e) cooked
cuite see cuit
cultivé(e) cultivated
culturel(le) cultural
culturelle see culturel

D

d' see de
d'accord OK
dans in/into
dans le nord in the north
la danse danse
le/la danseur/danseuse dancer
de l' some/of the (+ sing noun starting with a vowel)
de la some/of the (+ f sing noun)
de préférence preferably
de rien it's OK/not at all/don't mention it
de/d' (+ sing noun starting with a vowel) from/of
débarrasser to clear
débarrasser la table to clear the table
le début beginning
décembre December
la déception disappointment
les déchets (m plur) rubbish

déconnecter to disconnect
décourager to discourage
*découvrir to discover
défense de … don't …
dégoûtant(e) disgusting
dégueulasse gross (slang)
délicieuse see délicieux
délicieux(euse) delicious
demain tomorrow
la demi-heure half hour
le demi-litre half-litre
le départ departure
le dépliant leaflet
le dépôt paying in (at a bank)
déranger to bother
dernier/ère last
(il) se déroule (v. se dérouler) (it) takes place (unfolds)
se dérouler to take place (unfold)
derrière behind
des (= de + les) some/any/of the (+ plur noun)
désapprouver to disapprouve
le désavantage disadvantage
(vous) descendez (v. descendre) (you) go down
descendre to go down
désinfecter to disinfect
désirer to wish/to want
désolé(e) sorry
désolée see désolé
le dessert dessert
dessus on top
le dessus top
la destination destination
détruit(e) destroyed
deux two
deuxième second
devant in front of
*devenir to become
la déviation diversion
(il/elle) devient (v. *devenir) (he/she) becomes
*devoir to have to/to owe
diabétique (m/f) diabetic
(le) dimanche Sunday
dîné (v. dîner) had dinner
dîner to have dinner
*dire to say
la direction direction
le distributeur de billets ATM/cash machine
dit (v. *dire) said/told
(il/elle) dit (v. *dire) (he/she) says
dix ten
dix-huit eighteen
dix-neuf nineteen
dix-sept seventeen
(je) dois (v. *devoir) (I) owe/must
(il/elle) doit (*devoir) (he/she) must

donner un coup de main to give a hand
douce see *doux*
doux/douce soft/sweet
douze twelve
droite right
du (= de + le) some/of the *(+ m sing noun)*
dû *(v. *devoir)* had to

E

l' eau *(f)* water
l' échange *(m)* exchange
l' Écossais(e) Scotsman/woman
écossaise Scottish
l' écran *(m)* screen
*écrire to write
s' *écrire to be spelt (written)
eh bien … well …
elle she/it
elles they
l' embouteillage *(m)* traffic jam
emprunter to borrow
en in/of it/of them
en blanc in white
en bleu in blue
en face de opposite
en orange in orange
en seconde in standard class
en vacances on holiday
en voyage on a journey/trip
enchanté(e) delighted
enchantée see *enchanté*
encore again
l' endroit *(m)* place
l' enfant *(m/f)* child
entre between
l' entrée *(f)* entrance
l' enveloppe *(f)* envelope
l' épice *(f)* spice
l' épicerie *(f)* grocer's
l' équipe *(f)* team
(tu) es *(v. *être)* (you) are *(informal)*
espagnol(e) Spanish
*essayer to try/to try on
l' essence *(f)* petrol
*essuyer to dry (up)
(il/elle/on) est *(v. *être)* (he/she/it) is/(we) are
(il/elle) est constitué(e) de *(v. *être constitué(e) de)* (it) is made of
est-ce qu' see *est-ce que*
est-ce que/est-ce qu' … lit. 'is it that …' *(introduces a question)*
est-ce qu'il y a …? is there any …?/are there any …?
et and
et alors? so what?
et demie half past (the hour)

et quart quarter past (the hour)
et vous? and you?/how about you?/and you are?
l' été *(m)* summer
(vous) êtes *(v. *être)* (you) are *(formal)*
étranger(ère) stranger/foreigner
*être to be
*être constitué(e) de to be made up of
euh … erm …
l' euro *(m)* euro
excuser to excuse
excusez-moi ! *(v. excuser)* excuse-me
l' exemple *(m)* example
l' exploration *(f)* exploration
l' exposition *(f)* exhibition

F

la faim hunger
*faire to do/to make
*faire la vaisselle to do the washing up
*faire les courses to go shopping
*faire revenir to fry
*faire un régime to be on a diet
*faire un tour to go for a walk/a ride
(il/elle/on) fait *(v. *faire)* (he/she/it) does/makes (we) do/make
fait *(v. *faire)* done
(vous) faites *(v. *faire)* (you) do/make
(vous) faites revenir *(v. *faire revenir)* (you) fry
la famille family
la farine flour
fatigué(e) tired
félicitations! *(f plur)* congratulations!
la femme wife
(il/elle) ferme *(v. fermer)* (it) closes
fermer to close
(la) fermeture closing
le festival festival
la fête festival/fête
le feu fire/heat
les feux *(m plur)* traffic lights
le/la fiancé(e) fiancé(e)
fiancée see *fiancé*
la fille daughter
le film film
le fils son
fin(e) thin
fini *(v. finir)* finished
finir to finish/end
(il/elle) finit *(v. finir)* (it) ends
fixés see *les yeux fixés sur*
la fleur flower
la fois time
le fond bottom
la fontaine fountain
le foot football

la **forêt** forest
fou/folle mad
le **four** oven
la **fourchette** fork
(le) **français** French *(language)*
français(e) French
le/la **Français(e)** Frenchman/woman
française see *français*
Française see *Français*
froid(e) cold
le **fromage** cheese
la **fromagerie** cheese shop
(je) **fume** *(v. fumer)* (I) smoke
fumer to smoke
fumeur smoking

G

(le) **gallois** Welsh *(language)*
le/la **Gallois(e)** Welshman/woman
gallois(e) Welsh
la **gare** (railway) station
(la) **gauche** left
la **générosité** generosity
les **gens** *(m plur)* people
gentil(le) kind
le **golf** golf (course)
goûté *(v. goûter)* tasted
goûter to taste
le **gramme** gramme
grand(e) big
grande see *grand*
la **Grande-Bretagne** Great Britain
le **grand-père** grandfather
la **grenade** pomegranate
grillé(e) toasted
grillée see *grillé*
griller to grill
(vous) **grillez** *(v. griller)* (you) grill
la **grippe** flu
le **gruyère** Swiss cheese
le **guichet** ticket office

H

(j') **habite** *(v. habiter)* (I) live
habiter to live
(vous) **habitez** *(v. habiter)* (you) live
hebdomadaire weekly
hein? isn't it?
l' **heure** *(f)* hour/time
heureuse see *heureux*
heureux/euse happy
l' **histoire** *(f)* history/story
l' **homme** *(m)* man

l' **hôpital** *(m)* hospital
l' **horaire** *(m)* timetable
les **horaires** *(m plur)* timetable/times
l' **horreur** *(f)* horror
l' **hôtel** *(m)* hotel
l' **huile** *(f)* oil
huit eight
l' **huître** *(f)* oyster
l' **humoriste** *(m/f)* comedian

I

ici here
il he/it
il fait beau *(v. *faire)* the weather is good
il faut *(v. *falloir)* it is necessary/(I/you/we) need/must/
have to
il me faut *(v. *falloir)* I need
il m'en faut deux *(v. *falloir)* I need two
il vous faut *(v. *falloir)* (you) need
il y a there is/there are
il y a …? is there any …?/are there any …?
l' **île** *(f)* island
ils they
l' **imagination** *(f)* imagination
l' **imbécile** *(m/f)* idiot
immédiat(e) immediate
l' **impasse** *(f)* dead end/no through road
indiquer to show
l' **information** *(f)* information
l' **insecte** *(m)* insect
intéressant(e) interesting
intéressante see *intéressant*
(ça) **intéresse** *(v. intéresser)* (it) is interesting
intéresser to interest (someone)
l' **intérêt** *(m)* interest
invité *(v. inviter)* invited
inviter to invite
l' **Irlandais(e)** Irishman/woman
irlandais(e) Irish
l' **itinéraire** *(m)* route

J

j' see *je*
jamais never
le **jardin** garden
jauni(e) yellowing
je peux …? *(v. *pouvoir)* may I/can I …?
je vous dois combien? *(v. *devoir)* how much do I owe
you?
je vous en prie *(v. prier)* please do/don't mention it
je/j' I
j'en prends un(e) I'll have (take) one
(le) **jeudi** Thursday

joli(e) pretty
jolie see *joli*
le jouet toy
le/la joueur/euse player
le jour day
le jour férié holiday (Bank holiday)
le journal newspaper
le/la journaliste journalist
joyeux anniversaire! happy birthday!
joyeux/euse happy
juillet July
jusqu'à until
juste just

K

le kilo kilo

L

l' the/it (in front of a singular word starting with a vowel)
la the (*f sing*)/it
là there
la pièce each
laisser to leave
(vous) laissez (*v. laisser*) (you) leave
le lait milk
la langue language
le the (*m sing*)/it
légèrement lightly
lentement slowly/gently
les the (*plur*)/them
les yeux fixés sur staring at
la lettre lettre
(il/elle) se lève (*v. se lever*) (he/she/it) stands up
se lever to stand up
la librairie bookshop
libre (*m/f*) free
la limonade lemonade
le liquide liquid
*lire to read
la liste list
le litre litre
la littérature literature
la livre (= *500g*) pound
local(e) local
locale see *local*
la location rental
loin far
lors de during/at the time of
la lotte monkfish
louer to rent
(le) lundi Monday
la lune moon

M

m' see *me*
ma my (*f sing*)
le machin thingy
madame madam
mademoiselle miss
le magasin shop
le magazine magazine
magnifique (*m/f*) magnificent
la main hand
maintenant now
la mairie town hall
mais but
la maison house/home
malade (*m/f*) sick
(on) mange (*v. manger*) (we) eat
mangé (*v. manger*) eaten
manger to eat
(tu) manges (*v. manger*) (you) eat (*informal*)
(vous) mangez (*v. manger*) (you) eat
la mangue mango
la manifestation event
(il) manque (*v. manquer*) there is … missing
manquer to be missing
le marché market
(le) mardi Tuesday
le mari husband
marié(e) (*v. se marier*) married
mariée see *marié*
se marier to get married
marqué(e) indicated
marquer un but to score a goal
le match match
le match de foot football match
le matin morning
me/m' me/myself
mélanger to mix together
(vous) mélangez (*v. mélanger*) (you) mix together
le melon melon
même same
la menthe mint
le menu set menu
merci thank you
(le) mercredi Wednesday
la mère mother
mes my (*plur*)
mesdames ladies
le message message
la messagerie vocale voicemail
la messe church service
messieurs sirs
messieurs-dames ladies and gentlemen
(on) met (*v. *mettre*) (you) put
(il/elle) se met à (*v. *se mettre à*) (he/she/it) starts to

le **mètre** metre
(vous) **mettez** (v. *mettre) (you) put
*mettre to put
se ***mettre à** to start
*mettre le couvert to lay the table
midi midday
le **Midi** South of France
la **migration** migration
mince (m/f) thin
minéral(e) mineral
minérale see minéral
minuit midnight
mis (v. *mettre) put
mi-septembre mid-September
le **mistral** mistral (cold wind in the south of France)
mixer to liquidise
(vous) **mixez** (v. mixer) (you) liquidise
moi me
moins less
le **mois** month
mon my (m sing)
la **monnaie (de)** change (for)
monsieur sir
la **montagne** mountain
le **monument** monument/historic building
le **morceau** piece
le **mot** word
mouiller to moisten
la **moule** mussel
moyen(ne) medium/average
moyenne see moyen
le **multiplex** multiscreen cinema
mûr(e) ripe
le **musée** museum
le/la **musicien/enne** musician
la **musique** music

N

la **nation** nation
ne ... jamais never
ne ... pas/n' ... pas not
ne ... personne nobody
ne ... plus no more/no longer
ne ... que only
ne ... rien nothing
ne pas stationner no parking
nécessaire (m/f) necessary
n'est-ce pas? isn't it?
neuf nine
Noël Christmas
noir(e) black
le **nom** name
non no
non-fumeur non smoking

le **nord** north
nous we/us
nouveau/nouvelle (m/f sing)/**nouveaux/nouvelles** (m/f plur) new
le **numéro** number

O

obligatoire (m/f) compulsory
occupé(e) busy
l' **œil** (m)/**les yeux** (plur) eye(s)
l' **office** (m) **du tourisme** tourist office
l' **oignon** (m) onion
l' **olive** (f) olive
OM Olympique de Marseille (football team)
l' **omelette** (f) omelette
on you/we
on y va? (v. *aller) shall we go?
onze eleven
l' **option** (f) option
orange orange (colour)
l' **orange** (f) orange (fruit)
l' **organisation** (f) organisation
organisé(e) organised
organisée see organisé
ou or
où where
oui yes
l' **ours** (m) bear
ouvert(e) (v. *ouvrir) open
ouverte see ouvert
(il/elle) **ouvre** (v. *ouvrir) (he/she/it) opens
l' **ouvre-boîtes** (m) tin opener
*ouvrir to open

P

le **pain** bread
le **panneau** road sign
le **paquet** packet
par by
par exemple for example
le **parc** park
parce que because
par-dessus on top
le **parfum** flavour
parisien(ne) Parisian
le **parking** car park
(je) **parle** (v. parler) (I) speak
parlé (v. parler) spoken
parler to speak
(vous) **parlez** (v. parler) (you) speak
la **part** portion/piece
(il/elle) **part** (v. *partir) (he/she/it) leaves
partant de leaving from

le **participe passé** past participle

la **partie** part

*__partir__ to set off/to go away/to leave

pas de problème no problem

pas mal not bad

pas trop bon(ne) not too great

le **passage** passage

passé (v. passer) spent

le **passé composé** perfect (past) tense

le **passeport** passport

passer to spend/to pass

passer devant to go past

(vous) **passez** (v. passer) (you) spend/pass

passez-moi pass me

le **pastis** pastis (drink made with aniseed)

les **pâtes** (f plur) pasta

la **pâtisserie** cake shop

la **pauvreté** poverty

le **pays** country

le **pays de Galles** Wales

la **pêche** peach/fishing

pendant during/for

penser to think

(vous) **pensez** (v. penser) (you) think

(il/elle) **perd** (v. perdre) (he/she) loses

*__perdre__ to lose

le **père** father

perdu (v. *perdre) lost

la **personne** person

personne nobody/no-one

les **personnes** (f plur) people

la **pétanque** boules (game)

petit(e) small

petite see petit

la **petite cuillère** teaspoon

peu few/little

(on) **peut** (v. *pouvoir) (we/you) can

(je/tu) **peux** (v. *pouvoir) (I/you) can, may

la **pharmacie** chemist's

la **photocopieuse** photocopier

le/la **pianiste** pianist

la **pièce** piece/coin/room/each

la **piqûre** sting

la **piscine** swimming pool

la **piste** (pétanque) ground

la **place** square/seat

la **plage** beach

*__plaire__ to please

(il/elle) **plaît** (v. *plaire) (he/she/it) pleases

le **plan** map

le **plat** dish

le **plat du jour** dish of the day

plus more

le **poisson** fish

le **poivre** pepper (seasoning)

le **poivron** pepper (vegetable)

la **pomme** apple

la **pomme de terre** potato

le **pont** bridge

le **portail** gate

porter to carry

la **portière** (car) door

possible (m/f) possible

la **poubelle** bin

le **poulet** chicken

pour for/to

pour aller à …? how do I get to …?

pourquoi …? why …?

pousser to push

(vous) **pouvez** (v. *pouvoir) (you) may/(you) can

(je/il/elle) **préfère** (v. préférer) (I/he/she) prefer(s)

la **préférence** preference

(tu) **préfères** (v. préférer) (you) prefer

premier/ère first

première see premier

(il/elle/on) **prend** (v. *prendre) (he/she) takes/(we) take

*__prendre__ to take/to have

*__prendre un verre__ to have a drink

(je) **prends** (v. *prendre) (I) have/take

(vous) **prenez** (v. *prendre) (you) take/(you) have

préparer to prepare

près de near to

près d'ici near here

le/la **présentateur/trice** presenter

présentatrice see présentateur

(je) **présente** (v. présenter) (I) introduce

(je) me **présente** (v. se présenter) may (I) introduce myself

se **présenter** to introduce oneself

présenter to introduce

le **préservatif** condom

prêt(e) ready

prie see je vous en prie

prier to pray

le **prieuré** priory

pris (v. *prendre) taken/had

le **professeur** teacher

se **promener** to go for a walk

propre (m/f) clean

provençal(e) provençaux/provençales (plur) from Provence

provençaux see provençal

la **Provence** Provence

PSG Paris Saint-Germain (football team)

pu (v. *pouvoir) been able to

puis then

Q

le **quai** platform

la **qualité** quality

quand when
la quantité quantity
quarante forty
quarante-cinq forty five
quarante-huit forty eight
quarante-six forty six
quatorze fourteen
quatre four
quatre-vingts eighty
quatre-vingt-dix ninety
quatre-vingt-dix-neuf ninety nine
quatre-vingt-douze ninety two
quel/quelle (*m/f sing*) quels/quelles (*m/f plur*) what/which?
quelle see *quel*
quelque chose something
quelquefois sometimes
quelqu'un someone
qu'est-ce qu' see *qu'est-ce que*
qu'est-ce que … comme? what … in the way of?/what sort of …?
qu'est-ce que c'est? what is it?
qu'est-ce que/qu'est-ce qu' …? what …?
qui who
qui est à l'appareil? who is calling? (*on the phone*)
la quiche quiche
quinze fifteen

R

la radio radio
le raisin grapes
rapé(e) grated
rare (*m/f*) rare
le rayon department
recommander to recommend
recruter to recruit
reçu (*v. *recevoir*) received
réduit(e) reduced
(on) regarde (*v. regarder*) (we) watch/are watching
regarder to (have a) look (at)/to watch
le régime diet
la région region/area
la règle rule
(ils/elles) rejoignent (*v. *rejoindre*) (they) join/get to
*rejoindre to join/get to
remuer to stir
(vous) remuez (*v. remuer*) (you) stir
la rencontre meeting
rencontré (*v. rencontrer*) met
le renseignement (a piece of) information
répéter to repeat
(il/elle) répond (*v. répondre*) (he/she) replies
répondre to reply
réservé reserved/booked

réserver to reserve
le restaurant restaurant
le retour return
retourner to go back
(vous) retournez (*v. retourner*) (you) go back
(ils/elles) se retrouvent (*v. se retrouver*) (they) meet
se retrouver to meet
ri (*v. rire*) laughed
rien nothing
risqué(e) risky
risquée see *risqué*
le robinet tap
la rocade ring road
le rond-point roundabout
rose (*m/f*) pink
rouge (*m/f*) red
la route road
la rue street

S

s' see *se*
sachant (*v. *savoir*) knowing
(je) sais (*v. *savoir*) (I) know
la salade salad
sale (*m/f*) dirty
la salle room
la salle de bains bathroom
la salle de séjour living room/sitting room
salut! hi!
(le) samedi Saturday
sans without
la santé health
la sauce sauce
sauf except
(vous) savez (*v. *savoir*) (you) know
*savoir to know
le savon soap
sdb (*abbreviation of salle de bains*) bathroom
se/s' (*in front of a vowel*) himself/herself/itself/oneself
sec/sèche dry
sèche see *sec*
seize sixteen
le sel salt
la semaine week
le/la senior pensioner
le sens unique one way
sept seven
sept euros cinquante € 7.50
septembre September
(il/elle) sera (*v. *être*) (he/she/it) will be
la serviette serviette/towel
*servir to serve
seul(e) only/alone
le short shorts

si if
s'il vous plaît please
simple *(m/f)* simple
simplement simply
six six
la société society
la sœur sister
le soir evening
la soirée evening
soixante sixty
soixante-dix seventy
soixante-dix-huit seventy eight
soixante-quatorze seventy four
soixante-quatre sixty four
soixante-quinze seventy five
soixante-seize seventy six
soixante-six sixty six
soixante-trois sixty three
la solidarité solidarity
son his/her/its *(m sing)*
sonore see *bip sonore*
(ils/elles) sont *(v. *être)* (they) are
sorti *(v. *sortir)* gone out
la sortie exit
la soupe soup
le souvenir souvenir/memory
souvent often
la spécialité local speciality
splendide *(m/f)* splendid
le/la standardiste switchboard operator
stationner to park
la station-service petrol station
(je) suis *(v. *être)* (I) am
suivant(e) following
(vous) suivez *(v. *suivre)* (you) follow
suivi *(v. *suivre)* followed
*suivre to follow
super! great!
sur on

T

ta your *(f sing) (informal)*
la table table
la tache spot
les tagliatelles *(f plur)* tagliatelle
la taille size
le tambourin Provençal dance
le tarif rate/price
le tarif réduit discount
tchatcher to chit-chat
le tee-shirt T-shirt
la télé *(télévision)* telly
le téléphone telephone
téléphoner to ring up/to phone

la terrasse patio
la terre earth/soil
tes your *(plur) (informal)*
TGV (Train à Grande Vitesse) fast train
le thé tea
le théâtre theatre
le timbre stamp
tirer to pull
les toilettes *(f plur)* toilets
ton your *(m sing) (informal)*
le tour walk/ride
le tourisme tourism
le/la touriste tourist
tourner to turn
(vous) tournez *(v. tourner)* (you) turn
tous les jours every day
tout droit straight on
tout le monde everybody
tout près very close
tout simplement simply
tout(e)/tous/toutes *(plur)* all/every/any
la tradition tradition
le train train
le trajet journey
la tranche slice
le travail work
travaillé worked
(je) travaille *(v. travailler)* (I) work
travailler to work
les travaux *(m plur)* roadworks
treize thirteen
trente thirty
trente-trois thirty three
très very
très bien very well/OK
trois three
troisième third
la tromperie deception
trop too, too much
trouvé *(v. trouver)* found
se trouve *(v. se trouver)* is situated
(je) trouve *(v. trouver)* (I) find
se trouver to be situated
trouver to find
la truite trout
tu you *(informal)*
le type guy/bloke
typique *(m/f)* typical

U

un *(m)* a, one
un petit peu a little bit
un peu (de) a (bit) of
une *(f)* a, one

V

(on) **va** (v. *aller) (we) go/are going
les **vacances** (f plur) holidays
(je) **vais** (v. *aller) (I) go/am going
la **vaisselle** washing up
(tu) **vas** (you) go/are going (informal)
végétarien(ne) vegetarian
végétarienne see végétarien
(le) **vendredi** Friday
*venir to come
*venir de to come from, to have just (done)
venu (v. *venir) come
le **verre** glass
(vous) **verrez** (v. *voir) (you'll) see
verser to pour
(vous) **versez** (v. verser) (you) pour
vert(e) green
verte see vert
les **vêtements** (m plur) clothes
(on) **veut** (v. *vouloir) (we) want
(je/tu) **veux** (v. *vouloir) (I/you) want (informal)
la **viande** meat
vieille see vieux
(je) **viens (de)** (v. *venir) (I) come (from)
vieux/vieille old
le **village** village
la **ville** town
le **vin** wine
le **vinaigre** vinegar
vingt twenty
vingt-cinq twenty-five
vingt-deux twenty-two
vingt et un(e) twenty-one
vingt-huit twenty-eight
vingt-quatre twenty-four
vingt-sept twenty-seven
vingt-trois twenty-three
visité (v. visiter) visited
visiter to visit
vocale see messagerie vocale
voici ... this is .../here (it) is ...
voilà there you are/there (it) is ...
*voir to see
(je) **vois** (v. *voir) (I) see
la **voiture** (railway) coach/car
le **vol** flight
vos your (plur)
votre your (sing)
(je) **voudrais** (v. *vouloir) (I) would like
(on) **voudrait** (v. *vouloir) (we) would like
(vous) **voulez** (v. *vouloir) (you) want/would like
*vouloir to want
voulu (v. *vouloir) wanted
vous you

vous allez bien? are you well?
vous aussi you too
vous avez ...? have you got ...?
vous désirez? (v. désirer) what would you like?
le **voyage** travel/journey
vu (v. *voir) seen

W

le **wagon** railway coach/carriage

Y

y there
les **yeux** see œil

Z

zéro zero

*	irregular verb
(m)	masculine
(f)	feminine
(plur)	plural
(sing)	singular

A

a un (m)/une (f)
a little (bit of) un (petit) peu (de)
a quarter past et quart
activity l'activité (f)
adult l'adulte (m/f)
advance l'avance (f)
advice (a piece of) le conseil (m)
after après
afternoon l'après-midi (m or f)
again encore
against contre
all tout(e) (sing); tous/toutes (plur)
allergic to allergique à (m/f)
allergy l'allergie (f)
am I in the right place? c'est bien ici?
analyst l'analyste (m/f)
and et
and you are ...? et vous?
and you? et vous ?
antiques les antiquités (f plur)
any un/une (sing); des/tout(e)/tous/toutes (plur)
anything else? avec ça?
aperitif l'apéritif/apéro (m)
apple la pomme (f)
April avril
are you interested? ça vous intéresse?
are you OK? ça va bien? (see *aller)
area la région (f)
around autour
as comme
as well aussi
ascent l'ascension (f)
asparagus l'asperge (f)
at à
at (our) home chez nous
at home à la maison
at someone's place chez
at the au (+ m sing)/à la (+ f sing)/à l' (+ sing noun
  starting with a vowel or silent 'h'); aux (+ plur)
at the corner au coin
ATM le distributeur de billets (m)
authentic authentique (m/f)
avenue l'avenue (f)
avocado l'avocat (m)
away à (dix minutes/cent mètres)

B

baker's la boulangerie (f)
ball le ballon (m)
bank la banque (f)
Bank holiday le jour férié (m)
bar le bar (m)
barman le barman (m)
bath le bain (m)
bathroom la salle de bains (f)
be *être
be (thirty) *avoir (trente) ans
be called s' appeler
be hungry *avoir faim
be on a diet *faire un régime
beach la plage (f)
beach shoes les chaussures (f plur) de plage
bear l'ours (m)
beautiful beau/bel (before a vowel or silent 'h')/belle (sing);
  beaux/belles (plur)
because parce que
become *devenir
bedroom la chambre (f)
beef le bœuf (m)
beer la bière (f)
before avant
beginning le début (m)
behind derrière
believe *croire
between entre
beverage la boisson (f)
bicycle la bicyclette (f)/ le vélo (m)
big grand(e)
bin la poubelle (f)
birthday l'anniversaire (m)
biscuit le biscuit (m)
bistro le bistrot (m)
black noir(e)
blue bleu(e)
boat le bateau (m)
book réserver
bookshop la librairie (f)
borrow emprunter
bother déranger
bottle la bouteille (f)
bottom le fond (m)
boules (game) la pétanque (f)
boulevard le boulevard (m)
box la boîte (f)
bread le pain (m)
Brie le brie (m)
British britannique (m/f)
bus le bus (m)
busy occupé(e)
but mais
butcher's la boucherie (f)

butter le beurre *(m)*
buy acheter
by par
bye! ciao!/salut!

C

café le café *(m)*/bistrot *(m)*
cake shop la pâtisserie *(f)*
Camembert le camembert *(m)*
can I …? je peux …? *(v. *pouvoir)*
car la voiture *(f)*
car park le parking *(m)*
card la carte *(f)*
carrot la carotte *(f)*
carry porter
carry on continuer
castle le château *(m)*; les châteaux *(plur)*
Champagne le champagne *(m)*
champion le/la champion/ne
change (for) la monnaie (de) *(f)*
cheers!/to your good health! bonne santé!/à votre santé!/
  à la vôtre!
cheese le fromage *(m)*
cheese shop la fromagerie *(f)*
chef le chef *(m)*
chemist's la pharmacie *(f)*
cherry la cerise *(f)*
chicken le poulet *(m)*
child l'enfant *(m)*
Chinese (language) le Chinois *(m)*
Chinese man le Chinois *(m)*
Chinese woman/Chinese girl la Chinoise *(f)*
chocolate le chocolat *(m)*
choice le choix *(m)*
Christmas Noël
cinema le cinéma *(m)*
class la classe *(f)*
clean propre *(m/f)*
clear débarrasser
clear the table débarrasser la table
close fermer
closing la fermeture *(f)*
clothes les vêtements *(m plur)*
club le club *(m)*
code le code *(m)*
coffee le café *(m)*
coin la pièce *(f)*
cold froid(e)
colour la couleur *(f)*
come *venir
come from *venir de
comedian l'humoriste *(m/f)*
competition le concours *(m)*
compulsory obligatoire *(m/f)*
concert le concert *(m)*

congratulations! félicitations! *(f plur)*
contact contacter
control le contrôle *(m)*
cool cool
corner le coin *(m)*
country le pays *(m)*
countryside la campagne *(f)*
crisps les chips *(f plur)*
croûton le croûton *(m)*
cut couper

D

dairy shop la crémerie *(f)*
dance la danse *(f)*
dancer le/la danseur/danseuse
daughter la fille *(f)*
day le jour *(m)*
December décembre
delicatessen la charcuterie *(f)*
delicious délicieux(euse)
delighted enchanté(e)
department le rayon *(m)*
departure le départ *(m)*
dessert le dessert *(m)*
destination la destination *(f)*
diabetic diabétique
dial composer *(when using the telephone)*
diet le régime *(m)*
direction la direction *(f)*
dirty sale *(m/f)*
discount le tarif réduit *(m)*
discover découvrir
disgusting dégoûtant(e)
dish le plat *(m)*
dish of the day le plat du jour *(m)*
do *faire
do the washing up *faire la vaisselle
do you have …? avez-vous …?
dog le chien *(m)*
don't … défense de …
don't mention it de rien/je vous en prie
drink la boisson *(f)*
drink *boire
drinks list la carte *(f)* des boissons
dry sec/sèche
dry (up) *essuyer
duck le canard *(m)*
during/for pendant

E

eat manger
eight huit
eighteen dix-huit
eighty quatre-vingts

eleven onze
end le bout (m)/la fin (f)
end finir
England l'Angleterre (f)
English anglais(e)
Englishman l'Anglais (m)
Englishwoman l'Anglaise (f)
enjoy (bien) aimer
entrance l'entrée (f)
envelope l'enveloppe (f)
euro l'euro (m)
evening le soir (m)/la soirée (f)
event la manifestation (f)
every tout(e) (sing); tous/toutes (plur)
everybody tout le monde (m)
every day tous les jours (m plur)
example l'exemple (m)
except sauf
exchange l'échange (m)
excuse me excusez-moi! (v. excuser)
exhibition l'exposition (f)
exit la sortie (f)
expensive cher/chère
eye l'œil (m); les yeux (plur)

F

family la famille (f)
far loin
father le père (m)
festival le festival (m)
fête la fête (f)/le festival (m)
few peu
fifteen quinze
fifty cinquante
film le film (m)
find trouver
fine bien
finish finir
first premier/ère
fish le poisson (m)
five cinq
flavour le parfum (m)
flight le vol (m)
flower la fleur (f)
flu la grippe (f)
follow *suivre
food la cuisine (f)
football le foot (m)
football commentator le commentateur (m) de foot
football match le match (m) de foot
for example par exemple
for/to pour
foreigner l'étranger/ère
forest la forêt (f)
fork la fourchette (f)

forty quarante
fountain la fontaine (f)
four quatre
fourteen quatorze
free libre (m/f)
French français(e)
French (language) (le) français (m)
Frenchman le Français (m)
French stick la baguette (f)
Frenchwoman la Française (f)
Friday vendredi (m)
from/of de/d' (+ sing noun starting with a vowel)

G

garden le jardin (m)
garlic l'ail (m)
get married se marier
get nearer s' approcher
give a hand donner un coup de main
glass le verre (m)
go *aller
go ahead allez-y/vas-y (v. *aller)
go away *partir
go back retourner
go down descendre
go for a swim se baigner
go for a walk/a ride se promener/*faire un tour
go past passer devant
go shopping *faire les courses
goal le but (m)
golf (course) le golf (m)
good bon(ne)
good evening bonsoir
good luck! bonne chance!
good morning! bonjour!
goodbye au revoir
gramme le gramme (m)
grandfather le grand-père (m)
grapes le raisin (m)
grated râpé(e)
Great Britain la Grande-Bretagne (f)
great! super!
green vert(e)
grocer's l'épicerie (f)

H

half hour la demi-heure (f)
half past (six) (six heures) et demie
half-litre le demi-litre (m)
hand la main (f)
happy heureux/euse
happy birthday! joyeux anniversaire!
have *avoir/*prendre (for food and drinks)
have a drink *prendre un verre/*boire un coup (informal)

have a good trip! bon voyage!
have a nice day! bonne journée!
have a nice evening! bonne soirée!
have a pain *avoir mal
have dinner dîner
have just done something *venir de
have to *devoir
have you got ...? avez- vous ...?/vous avez ...?
he il
health la santé (f)
hello bonjour/allô (on the phone)
help aider
her son (m sing)/sa (f sing); ses (plur)
here ici
hi! salut !
his son (m sing)/sa (f sing); ses (plur)
history l'histoire (f)
holidays les vacances (f plur)
hospitable accueillant(e)
hospital l'hôpital (m)
hot chaud(e)
hotel l'hôtel (m)
hour l'heure (f)
house/home la maison (f)
how comment
how about you? et vous?
how are you? comment allez-vous? (formal)/
    comment ça va? (informal)
how do (I) get to ...? pour aller à ...?
how do you do? comment allez-vous?
how do you spell it? comment ça s'écrit? (v. *s'écrire)
how much do I owe you? je vous dois combien? (v. *devoir)
how much does that come to? ça fait combien? (v. *faire)
how much is it?/are they? c'est combien? (v. *être)
how much/how many? combien (de)?
how's it going? comment ça va?
huit eight
hundred cent
husband le mari (m)

I

I je/j'
I need il me faut (v. *falloir)
I would like je voudrais (v. *vouloir)
if si
I'll have one j'en prends un(e)
immediate immédiat(e)
in en/dans/au (+ m sing)/à la (+ f sing)/à l' (+ sing noun
    starting with a vowel or silent 'h'); aux (+ plur)
in front of devant
in standard class en seconde
in the country à la campagne
in the name of au nom de
in the north dans le nord
in the way of comme

information l'information (f)/le renseignement (m)
insect l'insecte (m)
interesting intéressant(e)
into dans
introduce présenter
introduce oneself se présenter
invite inviter
Irish irlandais(e)
Irishman l'Irlandais (m)
Irishwoman l'Irlandaise (f)
is it ...? c'est ...?/c'est bien ...? (v. *être)
is that right? c'est ça?
is/are there ...? est-ce qu'il y a ...?
isn't it? n'est-ce pas?
it il/elle/le/la/l'
it comes to ça fait (v. *faire)
it is c'est (v. *être)
it is necessary il faut (v. *falloir)
its son (m sing)/sa (f sing); ses (plur)
it's OK de rien/ça va

J

jar le bocal (m)
journalist le/la journaliste (m/f)
journey le trajet (m)
jug (of water) la carafe (f) (d'eau)
July juillet
just juste

K

kilo le kilo (m)
kind gentil(le)
kitchen la cuisine (f)
knife le couteau (m)
know *savoir

L

ladies mesdames
ladies and gentlemen messieurs-dames
language la langue (f)
last dernier/ère
lawyer l'avocat(e) (m/f)
lay the table *mettre le couvert
leaflet le dépliant (m)
leave laisser/*partir
left gauche (f)/à gauche
left luggage la consigne (f)
lemonade la limonade (f)
less moins
letter box la boîte à/aux lettres (f)
lettre la lettre (f)
library la bibliothèque (f)

lift l'ascenseur (m)
light clair(e)
light blue bleu clair
like aimer
list la liste (f)
literature la littérature (f)
litre le litre (m)
live habiter
local local(e)
look (at) regarder
look for chercher
lose perdre
lounge le salon (m)
love adorer/aimer
luck la chance (f)
luggage les bagages (m plur)

M

madam madame
magazine le magazine (m)
magnificent magnifique (m/f)
make *faire
man l'homme (m)
manage to do arriver à *faire
map le plan (m)
market le marché (m)
married marié(e) (v. se marier)
match le match (m)
may I ...? je peux ...? (v. *pouvoir)
me me/m' (in front of a vowel)/moi
meat la viande (f)
medium moyen(ne)
meet se retrouver
meeting la rencontre (f)
melon le melon (m)
menu la carte (f)/le menu (m) (set menu)
message le message (m)
metre le mètre (m)
mid-September mi-septembre
midday midi
midnight minuit
milk le lait (m)
mineral minéral(e)
mint la menthe (f)
miss mademoiselle (f)
Monday lundi (m)
money l'argent (m)
monkfish la lotte (f)
month le mois (m)
monument le monument (m)
more plus
morning le matin (m)
mother la mère (f)
mother-in-law la belle-mère (f)
mountain la montagne (f)

multiscreen cinema le multiplex (m)
museum le musée (m)
mushroom le champignon (m)
music la musique (f)
musician le/la musicien/enne (m/f)
mussel la moule (f)
my mon (m sing)/ma (f sing)/mes (plur)
my name is je m'appelle (v. *s'appeler)
myself me/m' (in front of a vowel)/moi

N

name le nom (m)
near/near here près/près d'ici
necessary nécessaire (m/f)
need *avoir besoin (de)
never jamais/ne ... jamais
new nouveau (m)/nouvelle (f); nouveaux/nouvelles (plur)
newspaper le journal (m)
next to à côté de
nice beau/bel (m before a vowel or silent 'h')/belle (f); beaux/belles (plur)
nine neuf
nineteen dix-neuf
ninety quatre-vingt-dix
no non
no longer ne ... plus
no more ne ... plus
no parking ne pas stationner
no problem pas de problème
nobody personne/ne ... personne
non smoking non-fumeur
North le nord (m)
not ne ... pas/ n' ... pas
not at all de rien
not bad pas mal
not too great pas trop bon(ne)
nothing rien/ne ... rien
now maintenant
number le numéro (m)

O

of de/d' (+ sing noun starting with a vowel)
of the du (+ m sing)/de la (+ f sing)/de l' (+ sing noun starting with a vowel or silent 'h'); des (+ plur)
office le bureau (m)
often souvent
oil l'huile (f)
OK ça va (v. *aller)/d'accord
old vieux/vieille
olive l'olive (f)
omelette l'omelette (f)
on sur
on holiday en vacances
on top par-dessus

one un (m)/une (f)
one way le sens unique (m)
one way ticket l'aller simple (m)
onion l'oignon (m)
only ne … que/seulement
open ouvert(e) (v. *ouvrir)
open *ouvrir
opposite en face de
or ou
orange l'orange (f)/orange (m/f) (colour)
other autre
oven le four (m)
owe *devoir
oyster l'huître (f)

P

packet le paquet (m)
pardon? comment?
park le parc (m)
park stationner
part la partie (f)/ la part (f)
partner le compagnon (m)/ la compagne (f)
pass (to) passer (à)
passage le passage (m)
passport le passeport (m)
pasta les pâtes (f plur)
patio la terrasse (f)
peach la pêche (f)
people les gens (m plur)/personnes (f plur)
pepper le poivron (m) (vegetable)/poivre (m) (seasoning)
person la personne (f)
petrol l'essence (f)
petrol station la station-service (f)
phone téléphoner
photocopier la photocopieuse (f)
pianist le/la pianiste (m/f)
piece le morceau (m)
pink rose (m/f)
place l'endroit/le couvert (m) (when laying the table)
plate l'assiette (f)
platform le quai (m)
player le joueur (m)/la joueuse (f)
please s'il vous plaît
please *plaire
please do je vous en prie
pomegranate la grenade (f)
possible possible (m/f)
potato la pomme de terre (f)
pound la livre (f) = 500 g
preferably de préférence
present le cadeau (m)
presenter le présentateur (m)/la présentatrice (f)
press *appuyer
pretty joli(e)
Provence la Provence

pull tirer
push pousser
put *mettre

Q

quiche la quiche (f)

R

radio la radio (f)
raw cru(e)
read *lire
ready prêt(e)
recommend recommander
red rouge (m/f)
region la région (f)
rent louer
rental la location (f)
repeat répéter
reserve réserver
restaurant le restaurant (m)
return le retour (m)
return ticket l'aller-retour (m)
ride le tour (m)
right droite (f)/à droite
right then! allez! (v. *aller)
right? alors?
ring road la rocade (f)
ring up téléphoner
ripe mûr(e)
road la route (f)
road sign le panneau (m)
roadworks les travaux (m plur)
room la salle (f)/chambre (f) (in a hotel)
roundabout le rond-point (m)
route l'itinéraire (m)

S

salad la salade (f)
salt le sel (m)
same même
Saturday samedi (m)
sauce la sauce (f)
say *dire
scoop la boule (f)
score a goal marquer un but
Scotsman l'Écossais (m)
Scotswoman l'Écossaise (f)
Scottish écossais(e)
screen l'écran (m)
seat la place (f)
second deuxième
see *voir

see you soon à bientôt
see you very soon à tout de suite
September septembre
serve *servir
serviette la serviette (f)
set off *partir
seven sept
seventeen dix-sept
seventy soixante-dix
she elle
shoe la chaussure (f)
shop le magasin (m)
shopping les courses (f plur)
shorts le short (m)
show indiquer
sick malade (m/f)
sights les monuments (m plur)
sir monsieur
sirs messieurs
sister la sœur (f)
sit s' *asseoir
sitting room la salle de séjour (f)
six six
sixteen seize
sixty soixante
size la taille (f)
slice la tranche (f)
slowly lentement
small petit(e)
smoke fumer
smoking fumeur (m)
so what? et alors?
so? alors ?
soap le savon (m)
some du (+ m sing)/de la (+ f sing)/de l' (+ sing noun starting with a vowel or silent 'h'); des (+ plur)
someone quelqu'un
something quelque chose
sometimes quelquefois
son le fils (m)
song le chant (m)/la chanson (f)
sorry désolé(e)
soup la soupe (f)
South of France le Midi (m)
souvenir le souvenir (m)
Spanish espagnol(e)
speak parler
spend passer
spice l'épice (f)
splendid splendide (m/f)
spoon/spoonful la cuillère (f)
square la place (f)
stamp le timbre (m)
stamp composter
start (to do) se mettre à (*faire)
station la gare (f)
sting la piqûre (f)

stop l'arrêt (m)
straight on tout droit
stranger l'étranger/ère (m/f)
street la rue (f)
summer l'été (m)
Sunday dimanche (m)
sweet le bonbon (m)
swim nager
swimming pool la piscine (f)
Swiss cheese le gruyère (m)
switchboard operator le/la standardiste (m/f)

T

table la table (f)
tagliatelle les tagliatelles (f plur)
take *prendre
tap le robinet (m)
taste goûter
tea le thé (m)
teacher le professeur (m)
team l'équipe (f)
telephone le téléphone (m)
telephone téléphoner
television la télévision/télé (f)
ten dix
thank you merci
that ça
that one celui-là (m)/celle-là (f)
that's OK c'est bon
that's right c'est ça
the le (m)/la (f)/l' (in front of a singular word starting with a vowel or silent 'h'); les (plur)
the weather is good il fait beau (v. *faire)
theatre le théâtre (m)
then alors/puis
there là/y
there is/there are il y a
there you are voilà
these are ce sont (v. *être)
they ils/elles
thin fin(e)/mince (m/f)
think penser/*croire
thirteen treize
thirty trente
this (before a noun) ce (m)/cette (f)/cet (before vowel if m noun)
this is voici
those ones ceux-là (m)/celles-là (f)
three trois
Thursday jeudi (m)
ticket le billet (m)
ticket office le guichet (m)
timetable l'horaire (m)/ les horaires (m plur)
tin la boîte (f)
tired fatigué(e)
to à/pour/à destination de

to the au (+ m sing)/à la (+ f sing)/à l' (+ sing noun starting with a vowel or silent 'h'); aux (+ plur)
to visit visiter
today aujourd'hui
toilets les toilettes (f plur)
tomorrow demain
tone le bip sonore (m) (on answering machine)
too aussi (as in 'also')/trop (as in 'too much')
too much trop
tourism le tourisme (m)
tourist le/la touriste (m/f)
tourist office l'office du tourisme (m)
towel la serviette (f)
town la ville (f)
town hall la mairie (f)
toy le jouet (m)
traffic jam l'embouteillage (m)
traffic lights les feux (m plur)
train le train (m)
trainers les baskets (m plur)
travel voyager
try (on) *essayer
T-shirt le tee-shirt (m)
Tuesday mardi (m)
turn tourner
twelve douze
twenty vingt
two deux
typical typique (m/f)

U

understand *comprendre
until jusqu'à
us nous

V

validate composter
vegetarian végétarien(ne)
very très
very well/OK très bien
village le village (m)
vinegar le vinaigre (m)
voicemail la messagerie vocale (f)

W

wait l'attente (f)
Wales le pays de Galles (m)
walk le tour (m)/la promenade (f)
want *vouloir
washing up la vaisselle (f)
watch regarder
water l'eau (f)

we nous/on
Wednesday mercredi (m)
week la semaine (f)
weekly hebdomadaire
welcome *accueillir
welcome desk l'accueil (m)
well bien/ben!/eh bien …/alors?
well, I mean … c'est à dire …
Welsh (language) (le) gallois (m)
Welshman le Gallois (m)
Welshwoman la Galloise (f)
what … in the way of?/what sort of …? qu'est-ce que … comme?
what …? qu'est-ce que/qu'est-ce qu' …?
what is …? c'est quoi …?
what is it? qu'est-ce que c'est ?
what time is it? quelle heure est-il?
what would you like? vous désirez? (v. désirer)
what? qu'est-ce que … ?/quel? (m)/quelle? (f); quels? (m plur)/quelles? (f plur) (with a noun)
when quand
where où
which? quel? (m)/quelle? (f); quels? (m plur)/quelles? (f plur)
white blanc/blanche
who qui
who is calling? c'est de la part de qui?/qui est à l'appareil?
why …? pourquoi …?
wife la femme (f)
will that be all? ce sera tout? (v. *être)
wine le vin (m)
wish désirer
with avec/au (+ m sing)/à la (+ f sing)/à l' (+ sing noun starting with a vowel or silent 'h'); aux (+ plur) (for food fillings)
without sans
word le mot (m)
work travailler
work le travail (m)
write *écrire

Y

year l'an (m)/ l'année (f)
yes oui
you vous (polite)/tu (informal)/on (informal plur)
your ton (m)/ta (f)/tes (plur) (informal)/votre(m/f sing); vos (m/f plur) (formal or talking to several people)

Keep speaking French!

If you'd like to carry on improving your French, BBC Active has a range of other resources to help you.

Get Into French is an award-winning complete self-study course on CD-ROM, supported by a book, audio CD and website. The ultimate interactive learning experience, this is a fun and engaging way to learn French. Create a virtual character and take part in fully-animated dialogues, in a variety of typical holiday situations from hotel to beach. *Pack contains: 2 x PC CD-ROMs, 144pp book, 60-min audio CD (£34.99)*

Concise and easy-to-use, this handy reference grammar provides clear and accessible examples illustrating the language as it's actually used. *128pp (£6.99)*

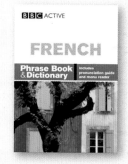

This compact book contains thousands of essential words and phrases to help you get the most from your trip. Also includes travel tips, menu-reader, and two-way mini dictionary, so you'll never be stuck for the right word. *224pp (£4.50)*

The French Experience is a highly successful beginners' course that reaches the equivalent of GSCE level. Its comprehensive approach develops your speaking, listening, reading and writing skills, and offers a valuable insight into French society and culture. *Pack contains: 288pp book, 4x70-min audio CDs or cassettes (£39.99) TV series regularly shown on BBC TWO, free on-line activities at www.bbc.co.uk/languages*

Don't stop now ...

Learn another language with the *Talk* series, available in French, German, Greek, Italian, Portuguese, Russian, Spanish and Japanese. These popular short courses for beginners will get you communicating with confidence fast. Interactive audio gives you the chance to practise the language, and there are six linked TV programmes shown regularly on BBC TWO Learning Zone.

Pack contains: 128pp book, 2x60-min audio CDs/cassettes (£14.99) Also available on DVD: Talk French and Talk Spanish (£19.99)

For more information, or to order any of our courses, go to **www.bbcactive.com**. BBC Active titles are also available in all good bookshops, and from BBC shop: www.bbcshop.com/08700 777 001.